Blue Moon Pizza
and
Rainbow Fire

Written and illustrated by:

Vivian Mattila Walikainen

Wedged between sisters and chickens,
truth and fiction, school and boys,
love and resentment,
laughter and tears:
Violet tells her story as she finds her way
through the ups and downs of life

Dear Reader,

I have considered you many times as I have been writing what started to be my story, but then became Violet's story. The growing up years are difficult for most people, but they are also some of the best years of our lives. We are shaped by the events that happen as we grow, as our mental patterns—frameworks for thinking—are developed. We take on ideas and patterns of living of which we are unaware at the time. Some are helpful and some are not.

All of us are born with dreams, talents, and natural gifting. Life and people shape us in ways that sometimes enhance those giftings and sometimes tears them down. It is our job, as adults, to examine our thoughts, words, and behaviors as to be the best possible influence for our children, and others in our lives. As younger people, we also get to decide what is truth and what is not. What feeds our soul and from what we need to run. We get to decide what we will take forward in life, or what must be exposed or left behind. And, that's part of the beauty of being human.

As I previously stated, this book started as a factual telling of my life. But, at times you need more to make a story. Sometimes a story needs to have some adventure breathed into it. And that is what I have done in this story. So, don't look for the people in my life, whom you may know, in this book. You will not find them as they were. But what you will find are characters who bear some resemblance to those in my past. Most of the events in this story also happened, but not typically in the way they are described in this story. Events and actions have been embellished and exaggerated.

Because a story is a story. A telling of life. Of the good and bad, the ups and downs. And the lessons learned. In this story, all that was done in exaggerated form.

This book is written to give hope to our children who may be struggling with purpose and identity, as Violet does. She seems to make so many agonizing mistakes and blunders. This book is written to help us better understand others—imperfect as we all are. This story is also written to help you, the reader, tell *your* story. Finally, this story is written to pay tribute to my past and the people in it.

Each of our stories are unique. Our own. My telling will be different from my siblings' stories. Each individual sees things from their own perspective, their own eyes. Eyes that have come to view the world in a unique way, based on personality, birth order, and circumstances.

So, this story is what I made of this tumultuous year of my life—the beginning of adolescence. It's a fictitious telling based on truth. And that is what life really is all about isn't it? It isn't so much about exactly what happened to us in life that is the ending point. It's the stories we tell. The stories we believe. It's what we make of what happened, the conclusions we draw about ourselves and our world.

This book took three years to write. During that time, I finished my bachelor's degree in Human Development. Those courses changed my perspective, my psyche. They mellowed me and helped me understand others and myself. To love myself and others. Through the process, I made peace with my past, and tied a happy bow on top. Just like a Christmas package. The wrapping may be a little weathered and crumpled. And the gift is a mystery. What did I put in the box? And how might it benefit me? How will I use it? And to me, that is a picture of life.

We each get to decide what to put to in the box that we carry with us. We get to decide how we are going to wrap it up. We get to decide if we will put a ribbon on top, or not. And we get to decide how many times we pack and unpack the box, what we put in and what we leave out. How many times we wrap and unwrap the contents. And how many times we change the cords with which we secure it. But the whole process is what makes us who we are.

I hope you are blessed by Violet and the story she wanted to tell.

Vivian Ruth Mattila Walikainen

Chapter 1

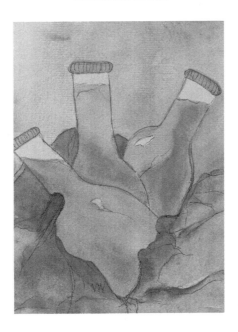

Homemade Root Beer, Blue Moon Pizza, and Rainbow Fire

Bam! The garage door banged shut behind her and Violet didn't care one bit. In fact, the bang made her feel just a little bit better. Silently grumping about her never-ending jobs of feeding bellowing cows and pecking chickens, Violet yanked off her barn jacket. She vowed never to own either beast when she grew up. Chores, chores, and more chores! Slopping chickens and wading through muck. Day after day. She could hardly stand it!

She jerked off her rubber boots and stood them up under the barn jackets that hung neatly on hooks in the garage. A place for everything. That's what her dad always said. A place for everything and everything in its place. She huffed and pulled off her hat, stuffing it into her jacket sleeve.

Clomping into the house, Violet washed her hands in the deep laundry sink and gazed out the window. A mama and baby deer were feeding in the pasture. Cool. She simmered down just a little bit as she watched them through the glass. Well, I guess there were a few advantages to being surrounded by trees and fields. Forget the muck and slop; there were other *good* things to think about. A cooling breeze coming in from the partially opened window blew across her face as she dried her hands.

Good things like soft summer nights spent sleeping under billions of stars. Especially when the Northern Lights danced in the sky. Now that was something spectacular! And, it *was* pretty cool to swing at the end of a long rope on the gunny-sack stuffed with hay in the huge hay shed, at the edge of the barnyard. Round and round and round—flying high and free! Oh, and going for a night swim in one of the nearby lakes. Yeah, okay. Country life wasn't so bad, all the time, 13-year-old Violet conceded.

Also, there were a few other advantages to rural living. Advantages like making (and drinking) root beer and eating store-bought pizza after a hard day's work. Well, you could make root beer and eat pizza anywhere, but to Violet, it seemed like a special event at the farm. Even though it happened only once in a blue moon for the family living in the big white farmhouse just past milepost 27 (as her dad often explained on the phone). Root beer and pizza were a rare occurrence for sure. And, Hannah, Violet's mom, had said both would be on the menu soon.

Summer times were times of planting and harvesting, but sometimes even the harvesting was over and it was time for some relaxing on the 65-acre farm, mused Violet as she gathered her socks from the sock bin.

The cattle farm was situated halfway down a long hill. A curved driveway, lined with evergreens swept up past the house to the barn and then continued on down to the backside of the house and the attached garage. Bushes and pretty flowers were scattered nicely around the perimeter of the

9

house. Bearded irises, smelling of root beer, marched up the driveway in the spring. A purple and white dancing parade. Wild pink roses and lavender lilacs grew profusely in their gardens.

Out through the barnyard were many outbuildings—homes to cattle, speckled chickens, and sometimes pigs. Pigs stink the worst, thought Violet. She definitely did not like squealing stinky pigs. Just the thought of them slithering in the sucking mud wrinkled Violet's nose.

But some people liked them.

Such as the girls who came to visit from New Hampshire. In fact, their mother had advised Hannah, "Don't tell Mary and Carla that you have pigs. They will want to ride them for sure!"

How gross! Little girls riding pigs! However, Violet *had* seen plenty others try to ride the dirty smelly hogs. And most of them ended up face first in the muck. Eww! Violet shivered at the thought of the pigs. She preferred to think of nicer things. Things like homemade root beer.

Yesterday, when Violet's mom had suggested making a batch of summertime root beer, Violet had already began tasting the fizzy sweet bubbles making their way into her mouth and down to her belly. She could hardly wait! So, she and her three younger sisters (Dinah, Eva, and Priscilla) and five-year old Israel had set to work. The two littler kids were still babies, so they didn't help much, but the rest of the children put their scavenging skills to use and gathered lots of glass pop bottles from around the farm, from neighbors, and even off the sides of the road. Because you could never have enough homemade root beer.

Violet and Lilith, who was a little older than Violet, had tromped through the pastures to a favorite spot to find old bottles. At the far edge of the back pasture, earlier residents had dumped garbage. Cool bottles, pieces of dishes, and old pots were dug up from among the decaying leaves. Violet had used some of these old jars for terrariums. She thought they were fantastic!

Early this morning, Hannah had overseen the washing of the large and small pop bottles, boiling them in water and setting them to dry on the counter. Then water, yeast, root beer flavoring, and a mountain of sugar was added to each jar. Finally, the bottles were sealed with fresh tabs, tightened down, and left cooling on the counter. Once cool, Violet and her sisters oh-so-carefully carried the bottles into the woodshed, just a short distance from the house. Stumbling over woodchips, the girls took much care to ensure safe delivery into the cool recesses of the shed. Violet and her Dinah nestled old grain sacks around the bottles, which were stored upside down to ensure proper mixing of all the ingredients. Now all that was left to do, was wait. And the waiting felt like an eternity!

That was this morning. Now, Violet was tired and ready for bed. Slowly, she gathered her missing socks, climbed the stairs, and continued getting ready for the night. Tiredness enveloped her. Wanting to sleep forever, she headed to her inviting bed.

However, on the way there, she was distracted by her image in the mirror. Stopping for a look into the glass that was attached to her bureau, she made a face. Baring her teeth and curling her lips, she exposed her gums. She was *so* glad the dentist had pulled her four eyeteeth last year. They had been *so* ugly, growing on top of the other teeth. She uncurled her lips and thought they were rather shapely. Gray-blue eyes looked back at her.

Dropping her gaze to her nose, she thought it was a bit too squishy. She poked it for good measure. Oh well. Overall, she thought she looked just fine. Her hair was long, a little curly and dirty blonde...What a dumb term—dirty blonde. Brownish-blonde, that's what she'd call it from now on.

Turning away from her image, Violet pulled on her pjs, climbed into her friendly bed, and thought about the root beer fermenting in the woodshed. Yum-my!

Even though it was only about a week that was needed to make root beer, the bottles needed checking on each day, according to vigilant Violet. Early the next morning, she crept into the dark, musty woodshed, thinking to maybe sample a small bottle, just one little bottle that she was sure no one would miss.

As she felt her way along over the woodchips in the semi-darkness, something soft and small land on her arm. Spider, her mind shrieked! Jerking around, she shot out of the woodshed, straight into her dad who was passing by, on his way into the house.

"Holy smokes!" he thundered, stumbling a little. "What in tarnation is going on?" Violet hardly heard him as she was jumping around, shaking her clothes and clawing her fingers through her hair. Spiders were the worst and the woodshed spiders were super creepy—all hairy and black. Just the thought of one crawling on her, sent her barreling into the house to get out of all of her clothes for a thorough inspection. "Spider! Wood shed. Root beer." Violet stammered over her shoulder.

By this time, her dad Adam had gathered himself and continued into the house. "Well" he mused. "Guess she learned her lesson. Doubt she'll try an early tasting of the root beer again."

Later that night at supper, Adam, from the head of the table, asked Violet how the root beer was coming along. "Just fine" she mumbled to her peas, potatoes, and roast beef. Adam gave Hannah a little smile; he then said that tomorrow night he was going to be cutting up some of the downed trees in the back pasture to prepare firewood for winter. The kids squealed.

"Can we ride in the trailer?" Eva shouted.

"And have a fire?" Priscilla chimed in.

"I don't see why not," Adam smiled at the young girls who shrieked even louder.

Violet thought her dad was really handsome when he smiled. In fact, the wedding picture and earlier pictures of both her parents showed them to be beautiful happy people. Their smiles were full of promise and hope.

The following evening, once chores were finished, Adam and the children loaded the chain saw, gas can, and axe into the rickety trailer that must have been red at some point in the distant past. None of the kids remembered the old wagon in its prime, but they didn't really care. In fact, they didn't even think about it. It was just the wood trailer, wooden sides cobbled together with a few screws and bailer twine. On a farm, you could pretty much do anything with bailer twine.

They piled in, a heap of old tennies, dirty jeans, and tattered work jackets. The children didn't notice their apparel either; they just noticed the smiles on their faces and the good feelings that made the smiles. Adam noticed too. He looked back as he bumped along on the old tractor. Out to the back pasture they went. A smile at his happy children further creased the lines of Adam's face. His worn work hat sat at a jaunty angle. Lifting his hat with one hand, he ran his fingers through his light brown hair, and then he replaced his hat, all in one familiar motion. His faded blue overalls crossed in the back; his barn shirt rumpled out of the openings. A stickler for safety, Adam never let the children get too wild around equipment, but he did understand that sometimes you just had to have a little fun.

And, that was just what the kids had riding in that trailer! In fact, they had a little more fun than Adam knew about, as the older girls jumped out and began running after the trailer. As Violet and Lilith ran to catch the trailer, the little kids howled. The trailer bounced over the ruts and rocked through the field. The older girls raced to catch up. Pigtails flopping, they bent down to grab the metal bumper of the trailer. Then they began riding across the field grass on their bellies. They all laughed, but kept their heads up, watching for cow pasties. That was the worst—riding straight through a fresh cow pie!

Luckily, the girls were paying attention and let go of the trailer before they were dragged through the cattle's fresh droppings. No sooner had they let go, than they were rolling to a standing position-running like maniacs to catch the bobbing trailer again. Too soon, the farm ride ended and Adam pulled the rickety trailer along the edge of the backfield. The kids piled out of the wagon, the fun was over and the work was about to begin.

However, this work really didn't feel like work at all. It was rather fun gathering the limbs as Adam cut them off the felled trees. Dragging the branches to a huge pile, the children worked on. Adam's chainsaw made little piles of sawdust that the younger kids gathered when Adam moved on to another branch.

Some of the children hauled branches to the burn pile and two others hauled the pieces Adam cut to the trailer. Lilith was stacking the wood on the trailer. Of course, she picks the easy job, Violet grumbled to herself. Actually, she didn't mind, less chance to run into the spiders that were always crawling in the wood, she reminded herself.

"Lilith can have them," she mumbled. Lilith was tall and delicate; blonde curly hair and bright blue eyes. She really was quite pretty, Violet thought grumpily.

"Well, pretty is as pretty does," Violet mumbled again, repeating a term Hannah often said. Violet couldn't decide if Lilith always *acted* pretty or not.

As Violet and her siblings worked, she took a moment and sat down on a stump. Mmm. The smell of fresh-cut wood filled her nose. She breathed deeply. I love summer, she thought happily. She took in the large field, the grasses eaten low by the hungry cattle. Evergreens and deciduous trees circled the large pasture. Back along the way they had come, a small creek wound its way through the property; it kept the cattle watered year-round. A gnarled apple tree with tons of apples stood watch at the first part of the field. A mature bent plum tree grew along another point at the edge of the meadow. Far-off mountains rose in the distance.

Violet could hear the murmur of water once Adam's chainsaw stopped buzzing. Down the deep canyon at the edge of the property, the water ran summer-lazy, freezing cold from the mountain-draining snow. On sizzling summer days, bees buzzing in their ears, the kids loved to tramp out across the field of grass and flowers, down into the deep gorge. Hanging onto sword ferns for support, they hurtled downward on the trail for a dip in the frigid water. However, the trip back up the steep trail made them just as hot and sweaty once they reached the top again. Somehow, it was still worth it.

Violet's attention was brought back to the stacked branches, as Adam torched the pile. The kids kept back as the flames leapt eagerly, flicking along the branches. Hissing and sparking, the fire reached for the darkening sky.

Then Adam told his children to watch closely as he took out his "magic colors" and threw a handful on the fire. The kids "oohed" and "ahhed." Blue, red, purple, yellow, orange, and green—all the colors of the rainbow—shimmered in the flames. It was stunning.

"Do it again!" the children chorused. So Adam the Magician threw more crystals into the fire. More "oohing" and "ahhing." And of course, more begging for Adam to do it yet again.

"No, we will save some for next time," Adam said, tucking his magic color can back into the tractor.

Eva, just turned nine, noticed movement in the field. Short, dark-haired Eva was like a furry kitten, soft and playful. "Hello mom!" Eva called as Hannah, Dinah, and the baby came bobbing across the field.

Hannah was wearing a homemade cotton dress, like usual. Tall and graceful, dark hair caught up in a bun, she jostled baby Daniel on her hip. Dinah, a year or so younger than Violet, had stayed back to help clean up supper and to pack up some snacks, which she carried in the picnic basket. As they approached, the children ran to meet them and began asking what was in the basket. Hot dogs and marshmallows.

All of the kids ran to find small branches to poke into the dogs and mallows. After loading their sticks, they crept around the fire, looking for safe places to brown their food. Faces turned away from the scorching heat, the kids lay low to the ground, where there was the least amount of warmth.

Seven-year-old Priscilla lost her dog in the fire and began to cry. Hannah offered her another. Wiping her blue eyes, Priscilla pushed her wispy brown hair back off her face. Sitting ever so carefully while this hot dog remained high on her stick, slowing sizzling. Soon it was nicely browned. Priscilla, face intent and dirt-smudged, began eating it off her stick. "Hot hot" she called out. Everyone laughed.

Then younger brother Israel, not to be out-done, began mimicking Priscilla. "Hot, hot,

hot" he hollered as he stuffed a blackened marshmallow in his mouth. Most of it ended up on his nose and chin, making the kids giggle again.

The family settled around the fire. Voices murmured. A peaceful breeze began to blow in the gathering dusk.

"Swing low, sweet chariot, coming for to carry me home," Adam's voice sang out softly across the field from where he leaned against the tractor. The kids listened quietly, a few joined in.

"Tell my friends I'm a-comin there too. . . comin for to carry me home." Adam then sang another verse softly as he gathered the wood chopping equipment.

Soon he called an end to the merriment and told the children to gather the rest of the food and gear, as it was almost dark, and they still needed to get back home. The trailer was now full of wood, so the family trudged behind the swaying load. Violet and Dinah took turns running ahead, trying to out-do each other and beat everyone else home.

Soon they were all back at the farmstead, washed up, and tucked into bed.

Adjusting her position in her squeaky bed, Violet smelled wood smoke in her hair and on her pillow. When she closed her eyes, the beautiful colors danced in the flames. She sighed deeply and fell asleep.

A couple days later, Hannah suggested they use the money saved from selling the extra cow milk to the neighbors, to pick up some pizzas and try out the root beer for supper. The kids practically bounced in glee. "Only once in a blue moon do we get pizza!" Eva shouted. "Yippee!"

Pizza from town was a rare luxury. Hurrying through their chores, the children waited for Hannah to come home from errands, with the pizza. Soon the big gold suburban came sweeping up the driveway, in a small cloud of summer dust. Violet was sure she could smell Canadian bacon and bubbling cheese in tomato sauce!

The children crowded around the vehicle as Hannah came to a stop. They struggled over one another, eager to carry the pizza into the house. "Get the other groceries too!" Hannah admonished as she unlatched the baby and carried him in.

As Hannah busied herself with washing her hands and taking care of the baby, the others laid out the pizza on the counter, pushing the groceries into the corner of the kitchen.

"Can we get the root beer?" Dinah yelled down the hall to Hannah. "Yes, go ahead, but please don't shout," Hannah corrected patiently.

Short and stout, Dinah was helpful and full of energy. Dinah and Violet shot out the door, shoving each other to reach the woodshed first. Violet conceded and let Dinah lead the way into the den of spiders. Each girl grabbed a bottle and charged back into the house.

"Where's the opener?" Violet yelled.

Three pairs of hands began rummaging through the silverware drawer, searching for the missing bottle opener. Victorious, Dinah held the opener aloft. Lilith jostled the bottle into position for opening.

"Over the sink!" Hannah called, entering the kitchen. Just in time too. The lid was released, Lilith shot the bottle over the sink, and sticky sweet root beer exploded into the air.

"Oops" said Lilith sheepishly, holding the still bubbling-over bottle.

"Well, catch what you can" Hannah advised. "And open the next one more slowly."

Lilith licked her fingers and tried opening another bottle. Success. Cups were filled and appreciative slurping sounds filled the air (along with a few loud burps).

Usually the family waited for Adam to come home before eating supper, but tonight was a special occasion. The children grabbed pieces of still-warm pizza right from the box and began chewing the cheesy crust in great gulps. The pizza was not piping hot, since it took 25 minutes to get home from the pizza shop, but the children did not care.

It was so delicious! Violet ate her first piece in an awful hurry, but then slowed down, savoring every bite of her second piece. Slowly, she licked the last of the root beer off her lips and tasted the remains of the pizza.

Root beer and blue moon pizza. Violet couldn't think of a better way to end a day on the farm.

Chapter Two

Woodcutting and Open Windows

Violet woke early and shivered in the cold room. Even in the summer, the mornings were usually cool. However, afternoons in the upstairs bedrooms of the old farmhouse were hot and a little stinky. Hot because it was summer and stinky because of all the bat pee under the eaves. Bat pee or something similarly disgusting. However, by morning, both the heat and the smell were gone.

Violet pulled her blanket up and tried to sleep for a few more minutes. Today, she was going to get wood in the mountains with her dad. Getting an early start on the day, they were doing barn chores even earlier than usual.

Violet was looking forward to the day, but also felt a little grumpy thinking about all the work that she was going to have to do. She really was lazy at heart, she supposed. How to get a few more winks of sleep is what concerned Violet now. She punched her pillow and settled back in. However, sleep evaded her, as her thoughts gained momentum.

Violet spent a lot of time with her father when he was home. She was his right-hand girl for greasing the trucks, fixing fences, and doing other odd jobs. Adam was always busy doing something. "I can rest in my grave," he was fond of saying.

Adam did not talk about his childhood often, but from the little he said about his mother, Violet had the idea she had been a pepper pot, or worse, she thought unkindly. Sometimes Adam's parents came to visit from the mid-West; it was fun to have them, but Violet was always a little afraid of her grandmother. However, she *was jolly*, at times—laughing with the kids. She also walked to the store with Violet and her sisters, even though it was two miles away. And she did send them fudge and knitted mittens for Christmas. So, Violet thought, I guess she's probably alright. I guess anybody can be a little grumpy at times.

Because of lasting effects of a childhood disease, Adam was able to go to college on a scholarship and obtained a degree in Forestry. He also worked in the kitchen at the college. He was super smart. Adam seemed to know how to do or fix anything. Sometimes he helped Violet's older siblings with their difficult math problems—the language of which boggled Violet's mind. He had a good brain, no doubt about that.

Through Adam's work in forestry, he developed friendships with numerous people in the community. They respected him and enjoyed working with him. With others, he always expressed himself in a quiet, convincing way. Sometimes these people stopped by the house for one reason or another. They told funny stories about Adam; at work, he was quite a comedian. One time a rather witchy woman requested a new work vehicle, so Adam put a broom in her office with a note attached that said, "Here's your new ride."

Violet's thoughts quickly faded to the back of her mind. Hearing Adam's footsteps on the steps, Violet called out softly, "I'm awake!" Her father stopped climbing and went back downstairs. Violet flopped the covers back, stretched, and began rummaging through a pile to find her clothes. It was rather difficult, since her clothes usually ended up in a huge heap on her bed, and then eventually landed on the floor. She finally found what she needed and quietly went down the stairs.

Calling "good morning" to Adam and Hannah who were in the kitchen, Violet headed to the garage. Something delicious was cooking, tantalizing her hungry stomach. After climbing into her boots and buttoning her jacket, she stepped out the garage door to start her morning chores.

Pulling the door shut, she noticed the ancient green hay truck sitting in front of the barn, all ready to go. Adam was always punctual and prepared. Last night, Violet had helped Adam put racks on the truck so they could use it to haul wood. She was excited about the coming day. The sky was so brilliantly blue, even at six in the morning. Soon they would be heading to the hills to make some firewood.

Quickly, Violet finished her chores and returned to the farmhouse for breakfast. Mmm, it smelled good!

Hannah had fried some of their homegrown pork sausage. Sausage made from stinky pigs. Violet scrunched her nose at the thought. Well, stinky pigs or not, the sausage was delicious! Hannah had also made a family favorite—krupsua. A Finnish breakfast pancake baked in a pan, then cut into squares, and eaten with syrup. It was yummy. A big glass of cold milk finished off Violet's feast.

Hannah was now sitting on her favorite stool by the breadboard that pulled out from under the counter. She was packing their lunch for the day—sandwiches, carrots, two apples, and cookies. Each item was carefully wrapped in waxed paper and folded into Adam's metal lunch box. They also took coffee in Adam's thermos and a jug of water.

Violet put her plate in the sink. "Good-bye mom!" Violet called. "Thanks for the lunch!" And, out the back porch door she ran, the door thumped close behind her.

Climbing in the old chugging truck, Violet felt a little apprehensive, wondering if the aged beater would be able to climb the steep mountain roads. Oh well, she thought, Dad knows what he's doing.

They drove far up in the hills to harvest some cedar from a clear-cut. Previously, the trees had been sold and what was left, Adam was able to harvest. He knew about these things from working for the Forest Service. After driving for about an hour up winding roads— the truck groaning and chuffing the whole way, they finally arrived. Adam had found the place he was looking for. He backed the big truck into a good position and cut the motor.

Silence. Complete silence. Violet slowly pushed her door open. She stretched and looked around. Scarred by the tree-removal equipment, the immediate grounds were torn up and stumps lay haphazardly. But, all around them, thousands of trees grew on the hills and in the valleys. Not thousands, millions, Violet corrected. She had never seen so many trees! Everywhere she looked, even way out across a deep ravine, the steep mountains were covered with deep-emerald trees. Wow! It was amazing; almost hard to take in. Sliding out of the truck, she banged the door shut.

Violet and her dad gathered equipment and set to work. The loud buzz of the saw shattered the sacred silence.

After Adam sawed up the huge pieces of sweet-smelling cedar into smaller chunks, Violet hoisted them into the back of the truck.

Bang! The first pieces clanged noisily on the bed of the truck. The empty space looked enormous once she started stacking the wood into it; it seemed it would take forever to fill it up. Violet groaned.

But as they worked quietly, Violet was happy. She liked being with her Dad, working together. Soon they stopped for a coffee and cookie break. Oatmeal raisin. A favorite-yum!

Again, Violet noticed the stillness and the quiet. The sun beat warmly down on them; she removed her work coat. Deep and pungent, the smell of the cedar filled her. Cautiously, a doe poked her head around a tree. Adam pointed out a furry little rabbit hopping near a log. The forest was peaceful.

"What could compare to all this?" Adam wondered aloud.

Violet thought it was pretty too.

Soon father and daughter went back to work. Once the truck was loaded, Violet and Adam climbed into the prehistoric vehicle and headed back down the mountains toward home. Violet nestled into the lumpy seat, pillowing her head against the metal doorframe with her work jacket. They jostled on down the mountain. Occasionally, an eyelid would be jarred open; other than that, Violet slept on.

Arriving home, the other children helped unload the cedar chunks into the woodshed.

Simon, Violet's older brother was going to the lake for a swim, so Violet asked if she could go. Adam said yes and off they went.

All around the lake were the ever-present fir trees, crowding up to the shores. Far up on a distant slope, Violet could see some houses perched on the edge of the lake. They looked as if they might tumble into the water. Sun glinted off the windows. Pretty place to live, but scary, decided Violet.

Charging off the dock, Simon and Violet plunged into the water. Yikes! It was freezing! However, after the hard day of work, a swim in the cold mountain water was refreshing. Like an otter, Violet swam. Turning and twisting in the water and then gracefully gliding up on a log.

Swimmers and boaters dotted the rippling water. The buzz of the motorized boats and friendly voices filled the air. Gas fumes from the boat's motors wafted in the breeze. Wood smoke from cooking fires drifted lazily in the summer air. Violet smelled hot dogs; saliva pooled in her mouth.

Lying in the sun, brother and sister soon dried. Violet ate the apple she had thrown into her bag. Usually she liked apples, but in comparison to a hot dog, it tasted like the cedar sawdust that had blown into her mouth earlier in the day.

The sun blazed on. Soon it was time to go home to do chores. Again.

That evening, as the sun was setting, Violet pushed aside her ruffled, fading bedroom curtains. She removed the window screen and quietly climbed out the dormer window. Carefully, she made her way around the corner and up to the top of the house. Toes dug into the warm sand-like shingles. Beauty surrounded her. Feeling tall and strong, she balanced on the ridge. She was a magnificent sleek bird ready for flight.

She imagined all kinds of wonderful things about to happen. She thought about when she would leave home. She always knew she wanted to go to exciting places, and do wonderful things. However, the thought of leaving also filled her with a profound sense of sadness. Opening the window to her future seemed exhilarating but also frightening. She wondered why life was so complicated. She shivered and turned back. Gone was the sun; the wind was starting to bluster in the evergreens. Violet crept back down the steep roof into her window, replaced the screen, and climbed into her soft bed.

Stretching with fatigue, she decided she would have to figure out her future some other day.

Chapter Three

Sunday Afternoon and Barnyard Chores

Violet lay on the braided rug gazing at the changing cloudscape through the branches that reached for the sky. The old rug scratched through her clothes. Her mind drifted like the fluffy clouds. That's the way I feel, she grumped to herself. Head full of giant, puffy ideas bumping into one another. Changing and wandering like ethereal smoke from a fire into. . . .What? (She liked that word—ethereal. She had read it in a book of poems. It was one of those words that invited imagination.)

 But, back to her changing thoughts about her life. She could not seem to make sense of things. Big questions seemed to overwhelm her thoughts more and more often. Her future seemed to call to her. She wondered where life would take her. She loved her home in the valley, but she longed to go places and do things—exciting things! Things that were waiting just over the top of the hill, away from the sprawling white farmhouse and the swarm of sisters and brothers.

Violet's mind continued to float as she gazed at the heavens, reveling in the warmth of the fading summer sun. Pulling the light blanket up over her body, she snuggled into her Sunday afternoon dreams, scratchy rug and all. She must have dozed off, since the next thing she was conscious of was the voice of her father calling, "Vi, time to get ready for chores."

Sleepily, she replied, "Yes Dad," and sat up, still feeling a little fuzzyheaded. The sun had disappeared behind the tall trees and no warmth remained in her light blanket. She shivered; Sunday naptime was over.

Sunday afternoons were a welcome time of rest for Violet and her large family. Living on a farm brought many fun times and adventures, but also plenty of work. Plenty. Hollering cattle, stinky pigs, and noisy chickens needed feeding twice a day. The cow had to be milked, gardens weeded, vegetables canned, floors swept, and clothes for many bodies needed to be folded, day in and day out. There was always something to be done. Therefore, lazy Sunday afternoons were a cherished time of rest and relaxation.

As Violet headed into the house, she heard the cattle behind the barns starting to bawl for their supper. "Good grief! I'm coming!" she roared back. Bolting into the house, she stashed her rug and blanket. Quickly she changed into her work clothes—old pants, shirt, jacket, hat, and barn boots.

Barn boots of all sizes lined up under a long row of worn work jackets in the garage. Hay stuck out of a few pockets and mud was clumped on the toes of some of the boots. The garage smelled earthy and damp. Each family member had his or her own pair of boots and you had better not grab someone else's by mistake! That was a sure way to start a commotion. However, Violet never tried to wear anyone else's boots for another reason—she hated the thought of putting her feet in someone else's stinky boots. Yuck!

Violet's chores had changed many times through the years, as an older sister and a brother grew up and were not part of the chore rotation any longer. She currently helped in the barn, took care of the chickens, and fed the young heifers and steers in what the family called "the loafer" or the loafing shed. All of the buildings on the farm had names—the barn, the loafer, the feeder, the back addition, the shop, the lean-to, the chicken house, and the woodshed. Mostly for storing and chopping wood, the woodshed was also occasionally used for switching an errant child.

Violet usually did not get into trouble, but she avoided the webby woodshed as much as possible. Spiders liked to make their homes in the wood and Violet did not like creepy spiders! The thought of them crawling down the back of her neck gave her the willies. In fact, that is why she always wore a hat when doing her chores. Well, the spiders, and to keep her hair from smelling like barn (she hated the smell of the cows in her hair).

Finished dressing, she crammed the blue hat firmly on her head. A piece of hay stuck her scalp and she yelped. "Tarnation!" she spluttered as she pulled the hat off and dug out the offending stalk of grass.

Before leaving the house, Violet grabbed the bucket of vegetable scraps from under the kitchen sink, being careful not to drop any potato peelings or eggshells onto the floor— her mother was a stickler about keeping the floor clean.

The family dog, Frisky, met Violet at the door and followed her. Violet walked up around the woodshed and through the barnyard, dust raised in little puffs under each step. As summer was fading into fall, the rains had not started yet, but soon the dust would turn into a sea of sucking, sticky mud. Glancing up at chicken house, she saw faded red paint, dirty windows, cobwebs, and some old, wooden stairs.

As she headed up the creaky steps into the chicken house, the smell of the chickens accosted her. Wow, they stunk! Chicken poop clung in clumps to the weathered stairs. "Stay out," she told Frisky, who liked to come into the chicken house and rile the hens. He gave Violet a wounded look and the padded away.

Taking a deep breath and pulling the neck of her shirt up over her nose, Violet pushed the door open and entered the musty building. The chickens were clucking and gathering at the inner door, waiting for their supper. They could not resist pecking at each other as they vied for position to get their hungry beaks into the vegetable rinds. Violet approached the door, removed the latch, and stepped into the chicken run.

The hens tripped her in their charge to get to the food. Violet stumbled as she tried to keep from landing face-first in shavings and chicken dung! Huffing in annoyance, she caught her balance, but the scraps flew like the chickens that were now squawking and flapping and putting up a loud ruckus. "Stupid chickens!" Violet exploded.

Snatching up the almost-empty bucket, she pushed the dividing door open and stomped into the furthest pen, stepping over the short separating wall. The door slammed shut behind her and a cloud of dust filled the musty air. Gaining the farthest pen, Violet banged the bucket on the feeding trough in an effort to dislodge the last few scraps for the hungry old hens.

These poor birds had seen better days. Feathers sticking out in odd angles, they teetered around on worn and ridged claws. Clucking, the hens peered bewilderedly through the wire that hung between the pens. Cocking their heads, which contained pea-sized brains, they peered around trying to make sense of what was going on. Eventually, the disheveled chickens waddled over to the trough and began pecking eagerly at the food scraps.

Violet shuffled back through the door over to a sack of grain stashed in an area fenced off from the pecking birds. As she unrolled the sack, a huge spider slide down the bag and rolled off her boot. Squelching the desire to scream, Violet stomped on the offensive creature. Hearing its crunchy squish, she scanned the bag for additional family members. Finding no other creepy-crawlies lurking in the folds of the sack, Violet dug the cup that was left in the bag into the grain and scattered it in the troughs for the now-gently clucking birds.

She grabbed the water cans from each pen and brought them outside for filling. Adam wanted fresh water daily for the chickens. He said, "If you take care of them properly, they would lay more eggs." But, sometimes the water cans looked clean enough to Violet, so she just added water without cleaning the water dispensers. Today the chickens had ruffled Violet's feathers and she did not think they deserved fresh water. She filled the cans and put them back into the pens. They could suffer with dirty water, for all she cared.

Violet then gathered all the eggs from the laying boxes and put them in her empty scrap bucket. Fortunately, the egg boxes were mostly clean and fresh, but occasionally there was some poop and hay stuck on the eggs that needed to be washed off. But, that was a job for one of her younger sisters. After setting the bucket aside, she locked the doors; glad the chicken chores were done for the night.

Climbing down the stairs, relieved to be done with the henhouse, she groaned as she remembered one last thing she needed to take care of. Good thing she did, otherwise some chickens might have disappeared in the night. The coyotes that lurked deep in the woods would be glad to take advantage of Violet's mistake. Sometimes she could hear the coyotes howling in the night; it sent shivers up her spine. Once they had even heard the shriek of what her dad said was a cougar.

Tiptoeing around the back of the shed, she opened the big chicken-yard gate, and crept up to the back of the coop, being carefully not to slide down the poopy chicken ladder. Quickly slamming the outside door, she locked in all the nosey hens for the night. The coyotes will have to find something else to fill their bellies tonight, she reflected. Every morning Violet opened the back door of the chicken house so the speckled hens and the one cocky rooster could run free in their yard, pecking for bugs and scratching in the dirt.

Violet grasped the bucket to bring the eggs into the house for washing. The reeking chickens were rather annoying, but Violet had to admit the chicks that hatched each spring sure were cute. Each year, her father picked a hen to become a brooder. Adam would put a dozen eggs into a box in a small pen in the chicken coop to see if the hen would sit on the eggs for two weeks so the farm would get a new batch of chicks. The hens usually cooperated and the family enjoyed watching the baby chicks change into soft yellow bundles of peeping joy.

The chickens not only produced eggs for the family's breakfast, but they also were meat for the supper table. Every few months, Hannah would tell Adam that the chicken supply was getting low in the freezer. So, Adam would pick out a few older hens, take them out to the chopping block, tie a string around their necks, have one of the kids hold the string down, and chop! Off came the chicken's head.

Tossed over the high garden fence (to keep it out of the manure in the barnyard), the dead chickens would continue to run around and squawk for a couple of minutes, even after their heads have been severed. It was the strangest thing to watch—kind of freaky if you had not seen it before—a mostly dead, squawking chicken, running around until it finally collapsed into a bloody heap. Violet shivered and made a face.

Walking past the chopping block in the barnyard, Violet continued to reminisce about chicken-killing time. After the chopping and squawking was over, it was time to pluck the feathers off the chickens. This was a job no one relished, but it was one of the many necessary tasks to be done. Hannah would boil up a big pot of water and dump it into a bucket ready for plucking. Clean newspapers were laid on the ground in the barnyard and the grisly job began. Grabbing a dead chicken by the knobby legs and dunking it into the bucket of steaming water, Violet would wiggle it around, pull it out, and quickly begin ripping off all of the feathers.

That is one of the most awful smells in the world—wet, dirty chicken feathers; the smell just lingered in the air and got in your mouth as you plucked. Sometimes Violet would dunk the chicken again, just to be sure it was clean and that all of the pesky little pin feathers had also been pulled out. Adam's job was to cut the chicken open and remove the still-warm innards. Finally, the clean chickens were brought into the house for one more washing before being cooked and eaten. It was quite a process.

Never part of the cooking of the chickens, Violet was glad Hannah took care of that. Hannah was a fantastic cook. The smells of the food at the table was always fabulous—no recollection of wet feathers was ever on Violet's mind as she devoured the savory dishes Hannah prepared.

After leaving the eggs by the garage door, thoughts of chickens slipped out of Violet's mind and she went back to the barnyard. She hurried past the chicken coop on her way to the loafing shed and the bellowing cattle. Climbing up the step, she unlatched the door, and entered the shed, caught by the smell of hay and fresh manure. Fortunately, the sweet smell of hay covered most of the nauseating smell of cattle poop.

She grabbed a bale and dragged it down a narrow alley right in front of the long manger. She had forgotten to wear gloves and the stubbly hay poked under her nails and ripped her cuticles. "Ouch and darn it!" she spluttered.

Mooing and poking their big heads through the bars in the manger, the cattle stuck their long tongues out in an effort to swipe a lick of hay. Violet ignored them as she got all of the bales ready for feeding. She then placed each bale into the manger, grabbed the knife off the window ledge (Adam always insisted on putting everything back into its place so it was ready the next time you needed it). She cut the orange bailer twine off the bales, pulled the twine out, and spread the fragrant hay for the happy cows. Gone was the mooing, only cheerful chomping and tail swishing remained as the cattle enjoyed their feast.

As Violet put the knife back on the dusty windowsill, she noticed the cuticle of her finger was bleeding. The sharp dry blades seemed to always find and pierce her skin. She gently swiped the blood on the inside of her jacket.

Violet folded the twine gingerly, trying to keep her wounded finger out of the way. Stuffing the twine into an old feed sack, Violet clomped out of the building and latched the door. She noticed the supply of bales was getting low in the shed; Adam would want to know so they could move some hay into the shed on Saturday. Swinging the door shut, Violet turned the latch into place and headed toward the grain truck.

Her heart started beating a little faster.

Getting two buckets of grain through two fences and covering 200 feet of ground on a diagonal from the shed where the cattle were busy eating hay, always filled Violet with a small sense of dread. The cattle loved their grain and usually came charging for it. She was glad the hay she had just given them distracted the beasts for the moment.

Snatching two five-gallon buckets that were sitting nearby, she set one in the wheelbarrow that was under a small door in the back of the grain truck. Sliding up the latch, grain and dust gushed out. The bucket filled quickly, she slammed down the latch and sneezed. Lifting the heavy bucket out of the wheelbarrow, she set the second one in its place and sneezed again.

She rubbed her nose on her sleeve, hoping the sneezing was over. She did not want to alert the enemy creatures to her presence. Two buckets now filled, Violet gripped one in each hand. Skinny arms strained at the effort. She sneezed again. Her arms jerked and a few kernels of grain splashed to the ground. Hungry starlings flew in to take advantage of Violet's mishap.

Hoisting the buckets, she lurched a few yards and set them by the first fence. Climbing through the fence herself, she turned slightly and looked toward the loafing shed. Good. The cattle were still in the shed eating hay.

Moving quietly, she struggled through a small unoccupied pasture and brought the buckets up to another fence—to enemy territory. She was a stealth warrior on mission. She crawled through again. This time, her jacket caught on the barbed wire. Dang! Backing up slowly, she untangled it, and finally got through.

One of the steers stuck his head out of the backside of the loafing shed. She had been seen! Nosey Steer mooed softly and started moving toward her. He was still about 200 feet away.

Oh no! With a surge of strength and courage, Violet quickly slid both buckets under the fence and placed them up into the feeding trough, ten feet away. Again, she was thankful that the rains had not yet come. Otherwise, her job would be twice as hard. Heaving herself up into the long wooden trough, she spread the grain quietly. Her heart threatened to beat right out of her chest—boom, boom, boom!

Finally done, Violet threw the buckets over the fence, jumped out of the trough, and slid through the barbwire; she was safe. Victorious.

Clutching the buckets, she banged them together. "Come boss!" she bellowed. "Come on, you heathen beasts! Your supper awaits!"

Nosey Steer was already on his way. His compatriots shot out the door, intent on the best part of their supper. One by one, or two by two, they thundered toward the trough in a cloud of dust. Charging and pushing each other, the twenty Holsteins jostled for position. Violet shivered. She hated the thought of being mowed over by those shoving fiends, even though they were not yet full-grown. Swinging the now-empty buckets, Violet tramped back through no-man's-land.

She scaled the final fence and returned the buckets to their place near the grain truck. Her heart finally slowed down to near normal. Mission accomplished for another day. . . One for Stealth-Warrior Violet, none for the beasts. She couldn't help swaggering just a little.

Violet knew the coming Saturday was already going to be a busy day with the de-horning that needed to done on some of the bigger steers. A few years ago, Adam had started using a burning tool to remove horns from the cattle when they were quite young. Everyone was glad the days of sawing horns off bigger cattle were over. However, sometimes the horns grew back and needed to be removed. No one looked forward to this awful job.

Violet shuddered as she thought of the process. The offending animal was roped— bellowing and raging—his head pulled through a slot in the manger and tied tight. Blood squirting everywhere, the horns were sawed off as quickly as possible. Quickly, a clotting agent was poured into the wound and the animal was released.

Wild with terror, the animals sometimes threw their bodies around and eventually went down into the manure, gasping for air. When the rope was released, the animal always recovered. No beasts had died yet at the end of a de-horning rope. Violet shuddered again. She was always glad when the older kids were home to help with that dreadful job.

Chores finished, Violet stopped to rinse her boots in the murky water bucket that was placed under the eaves of the shop to catch the rainwater. She only put her boot in so far, to avoid getting water in the hole that was near the top of her boot. She did not want to feel the frigid liquid rush into her boot and drench her foot!

Farm life was dirty work, but Adam and Hannah worked hard at helping their kids learn to keep the mud and manure outside. Brushing the hay off her coat, she took off her hat, and put it in the sleeve of her jacket, to be sure no one else wore it. She didn't like the thought of someone else's stinky head in her hat.

She knew she would be heading out to do more chores in the main barn after supper. Adam believed in teaching his children the value of responsibility and shared labor. So, he divided the chores up equally, on a daily rotation. The younger children often teamed up with the older ones to help as they were able.

Further thoughts of chores left Violet's mind as she entered the warm farmhouse. Wafting down the hall, the savory smells encouraged Violet to get cleaned up and ready for the supper meal.

She ran upstairs to change her clothes. Her stockinged feet slid on the worn wooden steps, but she caught herself on the rail before she fell. Washing her hands quickly in the upstairs bathroom, Violet rushed into her room to finish her homework. Glancing outside, she noticed the fluffy clouds were long gone from the sky.

Darkness was descending for the night.

Chapter Four

Making Hay

Haymaking was a big part of summers on the farm. With over 200 head of cattle that needed feeding through the winter, lots of hay must be baled and stored. Adam bought the hay from local farmers. The farmers cut and baled it, and then Adam and the kids would go and pick it up off the fields.

Battered and worn, three old hay trucks were used for the job. Once Adam and the children arrived at the field, Adam bolted a bale loader onto the side of the truck, and someone drove around the field gathering up the bales.

Adam's job was to be on the truck stacking the bales as they came off the loader.

The driver had to be consistent and smooth, in order not jerk the stacker off the truck. Today Adam was going to let Violet drive the truck for the first time. She used to have the job of rolling the bales into perfect lines for the loader to easily pick up. She remembered the past carefree years, running ahead of the truck, rolling the bales into rows. Stalks of grass stung her nail beds and soon her fingers bled if she forgot to wear gloves. Fingers curled at the memory.

Avoiding the heat of the day, the farmers picked up the hay after supper. Setting for the night, the sun was doing pretty things in the sky. Beautiful blue, the heavens were shot through with a rainbow of streaking colors. The smell of the cut hay made Violet feel alive and happy. The field stretched out all around her. Life seemed good. No, she didn't mind her bale rolling job at all.

But today, Violet had moved up to driver. She felt excited and grown-up! Once they arrived at the field, she positioned herself on the long seat in the olive green vehicle; she could hardly reach the pedals. The steering wheel felt solid in her hands, she was the helmswoman of a great vessel. Courageous and strong. She prepared for the maiden voyage.

Easing the truck into first gear, she slowly released the clutch. Instead of the anticipated smooth take-off, the truck lurched, coughed, spluttered, and died. Embarrassment rose in Violet's cheeks. "Try again," Adam called from the bed of the truck. Even though she couldn't see her dad she nodded and turned back to her task.

Moving the long stick shift into neutral, she put in the clutch, and cranked the key, giving some gas. The truck roared to life. Violet sighed in relief. "Now ease it into gear slowly," Adam advised. Violet did as she was told, gave an extra measure of gas and they were off! "Slow down!" Adam called, grabbing for the front rack of the truck.

Violet eased off the gas and began to position herself (she was now one with the green machine) to pick up her first row of bales. She slowed down to be sure not to miss them. Driving was much harder than it appeared, Violet thought frantically as they lurched over the bumpy field. Somehow, she was able to maneuver the vehicle to properly align it to pick up the bales. She clunked along;

everything was going smoothly. Soon the long row was ending; Violet saw the corner coming on too fast.

"Slow down!" Adam called loudly from the back. Violet could not see him, but knew the bales were flying off the loader fast and furiously.

She attempted to slow down, letting off the gas, and tapping the brake. She was also trying to make the corner, the steering wheel wet in her hands. She needed to align the bale loader to pick up the bales and keep the truck at a medium speed. Everything was happening too fast!

Violet braked madly in an effort to just slow down! She missed two of the bales and thumped over another. Her rump slid across the seat, she lost contact with the pedals. The truck lurched and . . . died.

Sweat slicked the steering wheel and also ran down Violet's sides. She tried not to cry. She knew Adam would be furious. Slowly she opened the door and tumbled out.

Adam was already off the truck. He was repositioning bales and glaring at Violet over his shoulder. His tobacco spittle dribbled down his chin. Dinah stopped her job of arranging the bales to watch Violet's humiliation, or so it seemed.

Once Adam was done, he turned to Violet and said, "Get back in and start it up," Violet did not want to, but knew there was no one else to drive. And she knew she couldn't stack the bales like Adam wanted on the back of the truck. He had a perfect system and was proud of the fact that he had never lost a bale on the road. He even had a particular way he tied down the load, using long ropes and two large metal rings. He made everything look tidy and easy.

Violet obeyed and slid her soggy rump across the torn seat and slumped at the wheel. Tears threatened, she could hardly see. Swiping her eyes, she turned the creature over and it roared to life. Easing the evil beast into gear, she let off the clutch and the monster died again. She could hardly believe it. It seemed Satan himself was had taken up residence in the motor of the Sinister Truck.

Finnish swear words flew out of her mouth, along with the family favorites, "Moron!" and "Less-off!" She couldn't take the time now to decide whether the vehicle was a moron, or less-off, so she let both rip as loud as she dared.

Once again, Violet started the ogre and this time she was able to get it to lumber down the field and picked up another row of bales without stalling. A corner loomed in the distance; Violet was terrified. "Please God," she mumbled and somehow made it around the corner.

She wiped her clammy palms on her pants and made her way to the next corner. Success again. Feeling confident, Violet picked up a little speed. In the rear view mirror, she saw the bales starting to soar off the loader once again. She tried to slow down, but braked too hard and the wicked monster gave up the ghost—again!

She drooped back against the seat and wished this nightmare were over! She expected to hear Adam's voice again, but all was silent. She eased forward and glanced in the rear view mirror to see him roaring toward her, his uneven gait and flapping shirt making him look like a wicked troll. She imagined steam rolling off his hunched shoulders.

Adam jerked the door open and told Violet to get out of the truck. She slid out and wished the ground would open up and receive her. Not knowing what to do, Violet stood there. The sweat dried and the tears stopped. Soon indignant anger filled her heart and her head. She looked away, far across the field to the distant hills.

As Adam fired up the truck, it lurched forward and he began to pick up bales. Soon he stopped the truck, intent on climbing on the back to do the stacking. Violet didn't know what she was supposed to do, so she continued to stand there, focusing on things far, far away.

As Adam positioned the bales on the back of the truck, Violet glanced over and it seemed the steam was dissipating from his bent work-hardened body. Finished, he mopped his face with a worn handkerchief and dropped down on the bales. Then he quietly stated, "I'm sorry Vi. The truck was in high axel, instead of low. That is why you were having so much trouble driving it. Go ahead and try again."

Understanding and relief coursed through Violet. The anger seeped out of her toes; she was flaccid with spent emotion. Limply she crawled back into the truck and finished her job. She was once again one with the tamed beast. Exhausted Helmswoman of the Mighty Hay Liner.

They finished the load and drove home in the gathering shadows.

The next day, they went to get the final load of the season off the field. This time they used a sister in the fleet of hay trucks. Painted red and black, the truck looked like a grand warrior. However, she was an old cantankerous warrior.

Arriving at the field, they rapidly filled the truck with the waiting bales. Adam had arranged for a young man from the church to meet him at the field to drive the truck, so there was no chance of a repeat of yesterday's disastrous maiden voyage for Violet. She was back to her easy job of rolling bales.

As they finished up and headed home, Adam outlined the plan they would use to keep the bad-tempered truck in line as they drove down the short, but curvy steep hills in their hometown.

Again, fear began to pool in Violet's palms and pits. She remembered yesterday's disaster and anticipated another battle with an angry monster. As they crested the hill and approached the first bend leading down through the town, Violet slid closer to Adam as earlier instructed. Fear and trepidation beaded on her lip.

She positioned her knee behind the long stick shifter in an effort to keep the ogre in gear. Adam was fighting the red and black beast at the wheel; the truck responded to the restraint by backfiring as loudly as she could. Great billows of fumes rose behind her as she swayed around the second corner and lumbered by the grocery store and post office, spitting and coughing all the way.

"Hold her!" Adam bellowed over the noise of the fiend. "I'm holding!" Violet shouted back, lean arms straining at the effort.

Violet tried ducking down as townspeople gawked and stopped loading their groceries into their rigs. A dog howled to the skies. The second sharp corner was also dealt with and soon the last curve came into view. Out of the corner of her eye, Violet saw the fire station with the firefighters standing outside, looking on. One raised a hand in feeble recognition.

Situated on the final bend, a saloon (and the ensuing drinking) had irritated Adam for years. As the black and crimson monster bore down on the curve and the place of carousing, the beast came unleashed and fought for freedom. She resisted all of Violet's efforts to hold her in gear. "Let it go!" Adam shouted over the din. Violet did so and slumped back to her side of the seat.

The monster gave one last mighty backfire and farted a final cloud of dirty fumes near the door of the saloon. Adam took the corner, eased the once-again tamed creature into gear, and glided out of town.

Violet glanced out her side-view window to see the bar patrons spilling into the street. Waving hands in efforts to dissipate the black cloud, they lifted their beers high (in salute, or anger, or to drink, Violet was not sure).

She swiped her dripping palms on her grubby pants and bowed back into the seat.

Upon arriving home, Adam backed the prehistoric warrior up into the old barn. The barn was almost filled with hay for the winter. Just this final load and they were done. One final hot, sticky, scratching load. Violet was not looking forward to the next half an hour. The kids at home soon gathered. They knew what they were supposed to do when the hay truck rolled up the driveway.

Dinah and Eva climbed up on the truck—
seven tiers high. The kids and Adam
positioned the old hay conveyer (Violet hoped
it wouldn't break down today). It shot almost
straight out, running from the truck to the high-
stacked hay in the barn. Plugged in, the
conveyor roared to life. The girls on the truck
carefully positioned the bales as they chugged
to Violet waiting on the end.

Using her knee, she boosted the bales up to
seven-year-old Priscilla, who rolled them to
Lilith. Lilith handed the bales up to Adam, as
he stooped to avoid bumping the ceiling of the
barn. On they worked through the dusty
sweltering heat. Dust, hay stalks, and sweat
churned in the tight air, sticking to necks and
arms. Stubble poked cuticles. The conveyer
clacked on.

Finally, the last bale of the season rode up the
conveyer belt into the barn. Someone pulled
the plug. Silence filled the barn. Too
exhausted to shout, the kids staggered out
into the light of the waning day. Gaining the
outside air, they breathed in relief. Violet and
Eva slumped against the sun-warmed
weathered barn.

Hannah had cold water in a gallon jug waiting. Parched, the kids poured water over their faces and down their throats. Frisky, hay speckling his white fur, strolled by for a pat and a rub.

"Good work, hay crew," Adam said, mopping his neck and making his way slowly to the door of the vehicle, intent on moving the truck back to its stall in the large shop.

"Can we go swimming?" Dinah asked Hannah, who had come to gather the jug and cups.

Looking at her sweating offspring, Hannah smiled wistfully. "I don't see why not."

Shedding shoes as they ran, the kids charged across the lawn and banged into the garage. Up in their rooms, shorts, tank tops, and flip-flops were thrown on. Stiff and smelling of summer sun, swim towels were pulled off the outside drying line. The hay crew piled into the yellow suburban. Sweat began drying on arms, sticky and itchy.

Lilith was at the wheel. Windows rolled down. The young hay crew whooped it up and flew down the driveway and out to the road. Squealing the tires (unusual for Lilith), the kids zoomed down the hill, across the big green bridge, and on to their favorite nighttime swimming spot.

Deserted, the dark water called. Parking near the top of the boat ramp, the sisters jumped out and ran, yowling like untamed nymphs. One by one, they sailed off the dock. Hitting the shadowy water, the hay crew-mermaids splashed in delight.

Haying was done for the season.

The girls swam in the gloaming, wild and free.

Chapter Five

Book Mobile, Reading Adventures, and Fairy Dust

Reaching for a book on the shelf, Violet breathed in the lovely smell of the bookmobile. The smooth book cover made a crinkling noise in her hand. Dust from the road settled on the smooth book jacket. It almost seemed like fairy dust—just a sprinkling of magical adventure. Intense summer sun beat down into the open doorway of the library on wheels—the bookmobile.

Rows and rows of adventures, journeys, and quests lined the shelves. Opening the book, the characters seemed to come alive in her hands as she scanned the page. The poetic words caught her attention:

"Summertime, oh summertime, pattern of life indelible, the fade proof lake, the woods unshatterable, the pasture with the sweet fern and the juniper forever and ever, summer without end." She glanced at the author, E.B. White.

She liked the cadence of those words in White's story, but she was a little unsure what "indelible" meant. Well, that's what dictionaries are for, she reasoned. Violet smiled, tucked the collection of short stories under her arm, and breathed deeply. She loved it all.

Every other week, the library sent the green bookmobile to a pullout in the road at milepost 26, just one mile up the road from the farm. The bookmobile brought books to the rural community. On this appointed library day, Hannah had piled all the kids into the golden chariot, along with their books to return.

Reading was a privilege enjoyed by the whole family.

Upon arriving at the designated spot, happy smiles and summer shorts tumbled out of the suburban, along with the returning books. Little kids and big kids squeezed up the stairs into the waiting cavern; journeys needed to be made.

"Good morning!" the cheerful library attendant had sung out.

A chorus of 'good mornings' answered. The kids handed in their used books and made their way to discover new reading treasures, directed by the helpful librarian.

Violet loved the 'Wizard of Oz' books, 'Island of the Blue Dolphin,' 'Wapootin,' and tons of biographies and fictitious tales of famous people and courageous animals. She appreciated reading their stories, getting into their lives.

In fact, she couldn't imagine anything more wonderful than traveling back in time, showing up in one of her stories. Grinning, she thought of jumping in a plane with Amelia Earhart or settling on the prairie with Laura Ingalls. Wouldn't that be something!

The aroma of the bookmobile was just as tangible as the adventures and struggles of the characters in her books. She breathed it in again. Warm and filling. The dust tickled her nose. A sneeze escaped. Then another. She squeezed her nose, hoping no more would follow.

Violet gathered a few more books, anticipating fresh reading pursuits. She hated when a book ended, she felt as if a wonderful ride had come to a screeching halt. The characters had moved on, but Violet was left behind, sadly waving farewell. Maybe that's why she immediately dove into another exciting journey, hot on the trail of one more literary escapade.

Much as Violet and the other kids liked to read, Lilith was the true bookworm of the family. She read everything. Twice, or three times, or more. She read late into the night, most every night. Crunched down on the floor, reading by the glow coming in under the door from the light in the hallway. Technically, she was obeying the "lights out" rule.

Yes, Violet felt a little crabby toward Lilith, who seemed to get a lot of attention in the family. Tall, serene, and beautiful. Everyone's favorite. She's perfect, Violet thought with envy. And Violet herself seemed to make so many mistakes. It was all so maddening!

Yes, Violet concluded, books sure are a good escape from sisters!

As the kids finished checking out their books, neighbors were arriving and looking around. Violet and her siblings said good-bye and loaded back into the car with Hannah. Doors slammed shut. Seatbelts lay unused on hot vinyl seats as reading treasures were opened. Journeys had begun.

Dust swirled around the vehicle as Hannah wheeled through the dry summer dirt for the short ride home.

Once back at the farm, kids and books disappeared to favorite reading alcoves or gathered in the living room. Sun streaked into the large room, dust particles hung in the air, summer-heavy and still. Even the cows were quiet for the afternoon.

Adventures called from the pages of their books . . . and the farm kids followed.

Chapter Six

Berry Picking

Violet's sleeping mind fought between slumber and consciousness. Slowly she came awake as Adam gently shook her shoulder. "Time to get up Vi," he said to the shadows and the half-sleeping Violet, who groaned and rolled over.

"It's still dark out," she mumbled into her soft pillow and smelled her morning breath. "Ewww" she turned her head out of the folds of the pillow.

"Morning comes early on the farm," Adam replied cheerfully. "Besides you girls start berry picking today."

Violet groaned again and started to sit up.

"See you in the barn," Adam gently continued and left the room.

Violet swung her legs over the side of the bed, trying to jostle her sleeping body to wakefulness. Her eyes refused to open. Yawning loudly, she slid off the bed and stood up little by little. Feeling her way in the semi-darkness, she stumbled to the bathroom and splashed water on her face. Her eyes popped open and her body started to respond. She brushed her teeth, did her toilet, dressed, and trudged down the steps, hearing her sisters also waking up in the cool of the morning.

The previous night, the girls had sat at the dining room table playing Chinese checkers and excitedly talking about all the money they would make picking strawberries. They decided they would order clothes and shoes from the JC Penney catalogue for school. Licking fingers, they turned the pages back and forth—clothes, shoes, and jackets. Besides, it was the time of the year for yard sales and the girls knew they would find treasures at their favorite ones, which they went to every year. They talked about the previous years' picking and wondered how this year would be the same and how it might be different. Going to bed early, they anticipated their early waking.

This morning the berry picking and moneymaking dreams seemed a little less sparkly. However, the kids were used to getting up and putting one foot in front of the other. And that is what they did.

Soon the girls had finished outside chores and had eaten the oatmeal Hannah had made for them. They quickly packed their lunches (also assisted by Hannah). Gathering jackets and hair bandanas, they piled into the suburban and soon their mom hustled out of the house to drive them down to the General Store two miles away.

The berry bus was waiting for them, looking all grumpy and gloomy. Daybreak still had not come as the girls climbed up the stairs into the rattly, discarded school bus. Since it was the first day, the bus was relatively clean, but soon dirt, berries, and crusts of food would litter the seats and floor.

The yellow and black bus bumped along in the growing light, picking up other weary country children, who clutched their lunch sacks. As it always seems to happen, the rowdy boys gathered in the back of the bus, Violet and her sisters knew to sit toward the front. School buses were bad enough, but crude jokes and bad language was rampant on the berry bus. Violet did not care to hear it.

The sun rose as the bus crested the final rise to the berry patch. Gazing out her window, Violet saw rows and rows of green strawberry plants. She also saw large berries waiting to be picked. Despite herself, Violet was excited. She and her sisters quietly competed all day, seeing who could pick the most berries and make the most money. Dinah, Lilith, and Violet were closely matched in their picking skills, so they seemed to take turns "winning."

The top "berry boss" as the leaders were called, knew the girls were good, fast pickers. Often after they had been picking for an hour or so, the leader would come find them and take them with a few other pickers to a different "better" place to pick berries to be sold in stores; these were the "commercial" berries. All the other berries were picked with stems off for the canary, but the "commercial" berries the girls usually picked were to be the best berries, with their cheerful green caps left on.

And that's what happened today. Fern, the top berry boss, approached them. "Good morning girls," she smiled. Her one gold-lined tooth twinkled. "Do you want to pick commercial today?"

"Yes!" the girls smiled back. Picking commercial was way easier and the girls made more money doing it. They grabbed their lunches off the bus and climbed into Fern's rig. Soon two other pickers who the girls remembered from last year's picking joined them.

Driving a short distance, they soon arrived at the commercial picking spot for the day. Fern had checked the berries ahead of time and knew where the biggest sweetest berries grew. She told the five pickers that she needed them to pick 125 flats of berries. The girls nodded and dollar signs started dancing in Violet's eyes.

When the vehicle came to a stop, Fern and the girls tumbled out with the cardboard flats, picking buckets, and their lunches. Fern left with a jolly wave and the girls were on their own.

Morning was just coming over the distant rows of the berry field, long rays of sunshine reached friendly arms. Tall shady trees lined the edges of the field and a dirt road circled it. The day promised to be a scotcher (as Adam often said). The girls grabbed four buckets each, tossed a few ahead of them in their rows and the race was on.

The "plunks" of the berries in their buckets soon were replaced by soft thuds as the buckets filled. It did not take long and bucket number one was heaping. Knowing she would pick about 50 buckets of berries that day, Violet thought, one down, 49 to go. The dew from the bushes seeped into Violet's pants, berries added crimson, and dirt added brown. Soon her pants were a sodden mess and her fingers looked the same.

Hours passed. Violet and the others picked on in the growing heat. Pants dried, hard and crusty. Coats were left in the shade by the filled flats of berries.

Kneeling in the dirt next to the row of berries, Violet leaned over the fat row to get the succulent berries on the far side. Her back screamed in agony. She eased back and decided to straddle the row, which she did for a time. Soon blood filled her head and started droning in her ears.

She pulled her leg back across the plants and sank down to her knees again, landing squarely on a large moldy berry. "Gross!" she hollered, gaining the attention of the other pickers.

"Just squashed a berry," she sang out. Maybe it was the heat, or the fact that she was closing in on bucket number 37, or just plain giddiness, but she started feeling a little sassy. Pushing her curly hair back under her bandana, she decided to sing a little made-up-as-she-went-along song, to the tune of "Oh my darling."

"Squashed a berry, squashed a berry, squashed a berry . . .Clementine. . . ." She drew out the "Clementine" long and loud.

The other girls laughed along and joined in with other made-up verses.

And so the day passed. Filled buckets, knees in berries, more songs, a quick bite to eat, a run to the outhouse, a splash of water from the jug and back to the picking. And more laughter.

Fern's vehicle finally appeared, signaling an end to their picking day. Too tired to give a glad shout, the girls worked together to finish a flat, gathered their belongings, and slid into the rig.

They bumped across the ruts in the field, gained the highway, and drove to meet the girls' bus.

"See you tomorrow!" Fern called.

"Ok" five tired girls responded, as they trudged up the stairs of the waiting bus.

Hot tiring berry picking was finally over. Until tomorrow.

Chapter Seven

Summer's Harvest, Fall in the Air

Violet woke up early Sunday morning, stretched in her bed and gazed out the frosty window. The first frost, she thought. Her toes had pushed through the covers and felt the cool air. I'm glad we are done getting the food out of the garden, she mused, pulling her toes back under the covers. She knew once the frost hit, all of the aboveground vegetables would wither. Thoughts of summer's end and the beginning of fall filled her mind.

Fall brought changes to the farm in the valley. The sun's rays grew longer and colder, hiding behind the trees surrounding the farm. The cattle must be brought home from summer pastures rented from friends, hunting season brought fresh venison, and the busyness of the summer harvest was over.

It was always a relief to be done weeding, picking vegetables and berries, and canning. However, once Violet got past her lazy thoughts, she knew that her family enjoyed all of the preparations for winter. Her mind wandered over the past few months of the summer harvest. Snuggling back down into the covers and gazing absently at the frosty patterns on the window, Violet's mind traveled.

Violet, her sisters, and some friends went to The Dalles in Oregon each summer with a lean old man from church named Alfred. At church, he seemed very strict and austere. His few strands of hair flew wild in the wind; shabby overalls, and work boots were his normal attire. However, the girls knew Alfred was just as much fun as anyone. By the time the daylong fruit-picking trip was over, the small group that went to The Dalles in Alfred's old van were good friends.

Each trip was different; sometimes they would pick cherries, other times it was peaches or apricots. Alfred got orders from the church people and the girls helped fill the orders. Once picking began, Violet enjoyed sitting high on a ladder in a tree, eating the juicy fruit, gazing at the cerulean sky, and calling out in fun to the others. Feelings of contentment would bubble up inside her. Life seemed as sweet as the juicy fruit.

Another expedition was the family's annual huckleberry picking trip to the mountains. Violet's father knew all the roads through the National Forest and the best places to pick huckleberries. On berry picking days, the family would get the morning chores done before the sun rose, pack a lunch, and head to the hills. After they had driven awhile, the roads got steeper and the guardrails disappeared. Cringing from the window, Violet tried not to look down the deep ravines as they drove along; it was scary to think of their bright yellow suburban hurtling down the mountain. Violet knew her father was a cautious driver, so she didn't worry about that too much; however, it was always a relief to get back to safer roads.

On the other hand, the scenery was absolutely stunning. Tall trees everywhere, gigantic hills, sparking rivers, deep gorges, a faultless sky. What perfection! Violet knew an awesome God had created a beautiful world.

When the family would finally arrive at a good huckleberry patch, they rolled out of the suburban and gathered buckets for filling. Huckleberries are so small; it seemed to take forever to fill a bucket—plunk, plunk, plunk. But when everyone's berries were dumped together into the big bowls that were sitting ready in the back of the rig, it looked like an almighty harvest—a brilliant sea of purple. The berries were so sweet and good; it was hard to stop eating them once you started. Enjoyed in jam and on pancakes, the berries were savored all year . . . or as long as they lasted.

Violet tried to fill her pail as quickly as she could. As she was picking, she remembered to stay close enough to the others so she wouldn't get lost. It was easy to keep wandering from bush to bush and then find yourself a long way from the others; however, stories of bears and coyotes kept all the children picking close to the vehicle.

At times, Adam was a joker, telling the young children that a pile of deer turds on the ground were huckleberries. He laughed as the children reached for the berries, but then had to quickly explain what they really were before the child's hand touched the pile. A lesson learned.

Another venture was gathering cascara bark. Violet's older brother, Simon, had various moneymaking ventures throughout the community. During the summer, he peeled bark off cascara trees, dried it, and brought it to a local grocer who sold it to a manufacturer. Careful to only take as much bark as the tree could stand to lose, Simon was a good woodsman. The children knew if they peeled the bark off all around the tree, it would die.

Violet liked to go with Simon and Frisky in the early damp mornings, tramping through the wooded acres on the farm to harvest the bark. Sun just peeking through the dense forest and twinkling in the trees, all was serene and glittery. They dragged big gunnysacks with them. Heavy with dew and bark, the sacks filled slowly. Upon return, they dumped the bark out on a piece of canvas in one of the barns and spread it out to dry. Violet also appreciated the money Simon paid her for helping.

The farm kids also picked tansies. Tansies are a proliferous plant that will take over fields if left on their own. They are a small jagged-leafed plant the first year. The second year, they grow into a tall plant with yellow flowers. When the flowers bloom, they scatter in the wind like wildflowers and plant themselves all over the place. Adam paid the children to sprinkle a weed killer on the small plants. Pulling the bigger plants out and putting them in a sack for burning, was a little harder work.

The few dollars earned seemed like a fortune! Especially when they went to the General Store for candy. Red Hots, Lemonheads, and Chico-Sticks were Violet's favorites. However, she was always careful to brush after a candy-eating streak. It was always a challenge to see if she could make it without tooth decay between dentist visits because her parents paid the children if they had no cavities.

Peach picking was especially fun. Violet loved it when the peaches were ready for harvest; it was a glorious time of the year. Violet and her siblings went with their mom to a nearby peach orchard to harvest their year's supply. Juicy and succulent, the peaches were best eaten right off the tree. Yummy! The peaches came off the trees easily and the preserving was not very difficult either. The family picked boxes and boxes of peaches to eat fresh and to prepare for winter. Some went into the freezer or jam, but most were canned in quart jars and lined up, row upon row on shelves in the enclosed back porch. Adam had made floor-to-ceiling shelves for all the canned goods. By summer's end, the shelves were over-flowing.

Hannah and the girls spent hours blanching, peeling, and cutting the peaches before they were put in the jars with sweet syrup. After that, they were put in a boiling water bath for a little while, taken out carefully, and placed on a wooden breadboard on the counter, waiting to cool. Once the jars were cool, they were washed free of any sticky residue and put in the back porch, ready for a late night snack. Violet also loved to cut up a peach to be eaten with cream and sugar while reading *The Reader's Digest* or *The Grit*.

Growing up without television, the children picked up a variety of books for entertainment. Even the encyclopedias were good reading, when accompanied with a fresh peach.

The Grit was an old-fashioned country newspaper that everyone enjoyed. When it came in the mail, the kids were eager to have his or her chance to read it. *The Reader's Digest* was also a family favorite. "It pays to enrich your word power" or "quotable quotes" were fun items to read and assimilate. The children tried to stump each other with the information they gleaned from their reading. Dinah was a whiz with words and board games; rarely did one get the better of her in word games. It was rather irritating.

Applesauce, green beans, cherries, strawberries, raspberries, pears, apricots, and corn were also frozen or canned for the winter. It seemed there was always a harvest to pick and prepare for future use. Violet and her siblings did their share of grumbling when another row of beans needed picking, but they sure enjoyed the canned beans with fresh bread and spaghetti! A promise of a trip to one of the lakes for a swim was also a great incentive to get the beans picked early in the day.

Carrots could be left in the ground and enjoyed fresh all winter long. Sometimes as Violet headed out to do her chores, she took a detour through the garden and grabbed a carrot from the ground, rubbed the dirt off it and shoved it in her mouth. Mmm. It tasted delicious and smelled luscious.

Snippets of these thoughts cascaded through Violet's mind as she gazed out the window at the frost-covered trees that were scraping the sky. Sundays were a welcome day on the farm. A body could lie around for a while without needing to get moving, long before the body wanted to move.

Violet knew her father and older brother would soon be out deer hunting as often as they could—before and after work and every Saturday morning. The thought of killing the timid deer that sometimes came to graze close to the house made Violet a little sad. But, she pushed those thoughts aside and tried to think of the help the meat would make on the dinner table. Violet did not really like deer meet, but she did enjoy the summer sausage or "makkara" as it was called in Finnish.

Violet's ancestors were mostly Finnish. Her family enjoyed some of the traditional Finn foods and customs. Saturday evening visiting and sauna taking was one such treasured custom. Since Violet's family did not have a sauna, the whole family would visit another family and use their sauna. Finishing the night by singing and having a snack, the family enjoyed their outing.

The saunas were usually made of sweet-smelling cedar and had two rooms—one for changing and the other for bathing. The bathing room had a wood-burning stove in one corner (fed from outside the building) and a shower or water hose next to it. There were wooden benches for taking steam; the higher the bench, the hotter the steam. The girls usually sauna-ed first, the boys and men later.

As Violet wallowed in her bed thinking; another favorite fall custom—gathering with friends for a Thanksgiving feast came to mind. She loved making decorations and gathering acorns and leaves for the celebration. She thought hungrily of the turkey, potatoes, and pies!

However, the ice crystals she saw on the window were calling to her now so she slid out of bed, scrounged through the pile of clothes that had ended up on the floor—again—and pulled on her clean work clothes.

Wanting to get outside and crack through the ice that she knew would be covering the puddles, she hurried. And, since her room was quite far from the stoves that warmed the house and garage, she moved even quicker to get into her shirt and pants! Creeping quietly, she padded down the stairs, slipped on her coat, hat, and boots in the garage and stepped out the door into the clean, crisp air.

The sights and smells of a new day thrilled her, especially a clear frosty day! She did a cartwheel (boots and all!) just for fun and because she felt so delicious. She blew into the icy air. Her breath hung like a misty cloud. Tail wagging, Frisky greeted her at the door.

Violet ambled up the slight incline, around the old moss-and-vine-covered woodshed, and on into the barnyard. Mt. St. Helens, majestic and glorious stood on the horizon. Fog hung in the valleys. The deep blue sky spoke of a gorgeous day to come. As she rounded the second corner of the woodshed, she noticed there were no animals in the barnyard, but the small wooden gate was still securely latched. Adam was careful about details and looked for ways to prevent the problems that arose when cattle escaped their pens. No one enjoyed chasing escaped cattle! Slipping through the gate, Violet took her time crunching through as many ice-covered puddles as possible.

Each groove and hoof print was filled with freezing water, creating thousands of miniature ponds. The ice tinkled so sweetly when broken, the shards making delicate patterns in the little puddles. Mesmerized,

Violet stuck her booted toes and chilly fingers into puddle after puddle.

By the time she finished cracking the ice, her fingers were red from cold, the sun was coming up, and it was time to do her chores. She quickly fed the chickens and cattle, stomped through a few more puddles, rinsed her boots, and ran into the house.

It was time to get ready for church.

Chapter Eight

Church, Friends, and a Horrible Surprise in the Bathroom

Sunday mornings were a whirlwind of activity. The family moved quickly through their chores and dressed as swiftly as possible. Violet's mother always made something good to eat; dishes were washed and left drying on the counter. If the family would be coming home to eat lunch, Violet's father would peel the potatoes so they could be put on to boil as soon as the family arrived back home. But, today they would be staying at church for lunch and then attending the afternoon service. Dessert, bread, and a casserole had been prepared yesterday and were waiting on the counter.

Today, the family planned to come home as soon as the afternoon service was over, leaving no additional time to play with friends. It irritated Violet that her whole life seemed to revolve around feeding smelly cows and stinky chickens. It seemed they could never stay at church like others and play all day; they always had to leave early to get the chores done.

Oh, she knew other farmers did the same thing, but others lived closer to the church and could come back for the evening service. It wasn't that Violet loved going to church. She actually thought it was rather long and boring. But, she hated leaving early all the time. At times, she felt excluded if she wasn't with her friends all the time. Then they had special memories that she did not share. Some friends, she thought in a fresh huff.

On this Sunday (and every Sunday), Violet's father was ready to go long before her mother. He drove the suburban out of the garage and up around to the front of the house and honked the horn. "Bronk! Bronk! Bronk!"

How annoying! Violet wondered why her mother never seemed to be ready to go on time. However, she knew her mother was busy packing the light blue "train case" with supplies for the baby, grabbing jackets for the younger kids, and getting the food organized to be taken to the church.

Violet remembered how her mother had once worn her "tossuts" (pronounced 'dousous') or house slippers to church! Leaving in a rush, she had forgotten to put on her church shoes! Of all things! On the other hand, it also annoyed Violet that her father sat in the vehicle and honked the horn. Big help that was!

Violet's mother was fond of telling a story about Violet when she was a little girl. Tired of waiting for Hannah to get ready, Violet had gathered Hannah's belongings and said, "Here's your shoes, here's your purse, now let's go, mother."

Finally, everyone was in the vehicle. Adam released the brake and they were off. Violet and her sisters started working on memorizing their Sunday school lessons. It was at least a 30-minute ride to church, so they knew they had plenty of time to study.

The roads were curvy and bumpy; a cramped ride filled with kids jostling for elbowroom in the bright yellow-gold suburban. Violet's mother began singing, as she often did. She thought it helped the children take their minds off their petty arguments. The old songs were both soothing and mournful; many had been translated from the Finnish language. Today he didn't, but sometimes Adam would join in the singing with Hannah.

Arriving at church, Violet noticed they were the first ones in the parking lot. Nothing new there, she mused. Her father took great measures to be everywhere early, or on time.

Traipsing into the chilly church, Violet found a seat and settled down for the Sunday school lesson. Soon others arrived. Violet tried to pay attention as the long History lesson was read and explained. After that, the kids went to their grade level classes for recitation of lessons and more instructions. Then came the break. Finally!

Violet rushed outside to visit with her friends for a while before trudging back into the church for the regular service. Violet's family always sat two benches up from the back on the right side of the church. As usual, Adam got up and began helping people find places to sit as the church filled up. He was a self-appointed usher. The young men who liked to lurk along the basement steps avoided being corralled into church. Sometimes, they stood their ground and would not budge when Adam offered to find them a seat.

As the family settled into the hard bench for the service, Gloria nestled next to Hannah; her nose practically in Hannah's armpit.

"Mom" she whispered loudly. "It smells here." Hannah went red with embarrassment, hoping no one had heard. Good grief! thought Violet. What next?!

After the songs and prayer, the ancient preacher began his sermon in a sing-songy tone that seemed to go on forever—quivering and shaking. It was hard to pay attention to what he was saying, so Violet spent her time looking around at what others were doing. Moms were always going out with babies. Violet wondered if babies did much besides cry and poop.

Big boys on the backbench were snickering, and there was usually someone nodding off to sleep. It was funny to watch their heads bob up and down. The sing-songy preaching went on and on, punctuated by an occasional elevation in tone and then some loud honking into a handkerchief that seemed to get used past capacity. Gross! Violet tried not to think about it.

Turning her head, Violet gazed at the sky outside the windows. Tall and curved, the windows were beautiful. Violet noticed that the trees had only a few leaves left on them and there were just a few puffy clouds in the sky. The branches waved in the wind; Violet felt like waving back. She hoped the sun would continue to shine through lunchtime. She was not looking forward to the rainy season she knew was coming soon.

Savory aromas wound their way up the stairs to Violet's nose. It smelled so good and breakfast seemed a long time ago! Once the final song was over, everyone else got up and headed down into the basement for lunch. Adam insisted the family wait until the end to get in line to eat. Something about humility and esteeming others better than self. By the time they got their plates, there were only brown beans and a few hard scraps of some casseroles left in the pans. It figures, she groused.

Gross! Orange jello with raisins and shredded carrots. Who ate that stuff anyway?! Just the thought of the combined textures made her shiver. She was glad when she spotted the red jello with whipped cream on top. Her mom had brought some yummy looking pies that were long gone.

Once lunch was over, the kids were free to play in the churchyard as the adults visited. Violet found her cousin Lucy and they ran off to play. Soon Molly joined them. They all decided to go sit in Lucy's parents' car to talk.

As they were talking, they noticed some young boys following a man, named Jacob, as he walked around and around the church, his hands tucked into his pockets. Jacob had a very large head from birth. He smiled a lot, but did not talk much. The boys seemed to be making fun of Jacob, who started to run away. This only made the boys laugh harder and run faster. Violet was relieved when one of the adults noticed and made the boys stop the chase.

Chatting about important things, the girls exchanged notes they had written to each other during the previous service. Each was folded in an intricate pattern. Violet put her notes into her little black purse; she would read them during the next service. The purse was a gift from her father, bought during his last fire-fighting trip to Mexico. She loved her purse with the pretty wooden handles. It was fun when her dad came home from fighting fires with the Forest Service. He always brought special things with him.

Church was starting again, so the friends went in to go to the bathroom and then joined their families in their pews. Tired, Violet slouched over on her shoulder and went to sleep. She awoke to a baby squalling and she realized she needed to go to the bathroom again. Her parents did not like the kids going in and out of church, but sometimes it was necessary.

She asked her father if she could go use the restroom, he nodded his head and motioned for her to go. Carefully stepping around all the legs and feet, she was finally out in the aisle. As she went down the wide stairs, she noticed many young men sitting or standing along the edges of the stairway. Holding herself carefully, Violet made her way down the stairs. Thankfully, she made it safely down and entered the girls' bathroom. Blech! The bathroom stunk like old sewer water.

There were three separate toilets with doors that clanged as they shut. Violet decided to use the last one since it had the most room. Sitting down on the toilet, she heard a noise above her and glanced up. She was horrified to notice an older girl Nellie holding a camera and looking down at her! The girl must be standing on the toilet, Violet thought. But, why is she taking a picture of me? What in the world?!

As these thoughts crashed through her mind, the camera flashed and then the girl was gone. Violet was in a daze as she washed her hands and left the bathroom. She wondered how much the picture would reveal of her backside.

For the rest of the service, she was very angry and embarrassed, wondering why that horrible, stinking, mean Nellie would do that to her. She also wondered who else would see the picture! She could not get it out of her mind. What a horrid thing to do! Violet fumed and fidgeted on the hard bench.

Violet noticed Adam was offering the other children round pink mints. Whispering a 'thank-you' she popped one in her mouth. Soft and sweet, it melted on her tongue as Violet tried to concentrate on the sermon.

Soon church ended. The family gathered their belongings, quickly rushed into the car, and left the church—heading home to feed the hungry animals. Violet wondered why the cattle needed to eat so much, since they had more than one stomach. Seems like they could store some for later, she thought. She also thought about bringing some fresh cow poop and leaving it and a note, "For Nellie" by Nellie's car next Sunday. How would she like that?!

As they were driving out of the churchyard, Hannah sighed and asked three-year-old Gloria, "Why in the world did you announce to the whole congregation that my armpit smelled?"

Smiling sweetly, little angelic Gloria replied happily, "Oh, it was a nice smell, Mommy, like powder."

Chapter Nine

Saturday Sauna with Best Friends

"It's Tradition!" Sharon shouted with a smile.

Looking up from her dolls, Priscilla had just asked, "Why are we going to take a bath at someone else's house?"

Tonight was sauna night—Saturday—it was customary for Finns to visit those who had saunas. Plans were made to go to their aunt and uncle's house for coffee, visiting, and sauna. Priscilla might have been confused, but Violet was happy. She liked going to visit her cousin Ann. Ann's dad was rather scary, but it was pretty easy to avoid him, Violet mused.

.

The Scandinavians believe they created this wonderful way of relaxing and bathing—in a "sow-naa." Ann's sauna was a two-room small building, with an outer room frigid in the winter, and an inner room blistering any time of year, when lit by a roaring fire. The outer room was small, with clean rag rugs on the floor, benches along the walls, a high shelf stacked with towels, and a dim light secured to the ceiling.

The elders in her family and church seemed to find satisfaction in connecting with their past through traditions and then teaching these traditions to their children. Some traditions were passed down for generations while others were created more spontaneously. Either way, these familiar customs became central points of family celebrations.

 For Violet's family, these traditions involved physical activities, food, songs, and the use of unique language. Some traditions seemed awkward and strange. Others created sweet patterns of living. Patterns that created the framework for life and memories, Violet mused. And love, she added. Life, love, and memories. She was thinking back to the stories she was reading between chores and schoolwork.

Another favored tradition was making pasties—well, actually not making them, since it took a lot of time, but eating them. The Finnish pasties were made of beef, potatoes, carrots, rutabagas, onion, salt, and pepper all mixed together and put in individual piecrusts; then they baked for an hour.

Violet and her siblings were excited on this Saturday morning when Hannah announced she was making pasties. The girls started washing, peeling, and cutting the vegetables, while Hannah made the crust.

When everything was ready, Hannah rolled a small ball of dough into a circle; she carefully scooped on a heaping cup of the beef and vegetable mixture and then rolled half of the dough over onto the other half and sealed the edge. She repeated this until all the pans were full and there were enough pasties for supper and lunch tomorrow. Pasties were a treat and everyone loved them, especially if eaten warm with ketchup.

"Are the pasties done?" Dinah and Violet chimed as they came into the kitchen after completing their afternoon chores.

"Yes, get washed up and we can eat," Hannah replied from behind a pile of clothes she was folding at the table. Hannah gathered the clothes and deposited them onto the living room couch; Dinah set the table for supper.

When bellies were full, some children cleaned the kitchen. Adam and two others headed outside to finish the barn chores.

Later, arriving at Ann's, the children ran out of the house to meet Violet and her family. Smiles and greetings were shared and the brown woven sauna bag was deposited in the wooden sauna. Smoke was blowing in the wind as it puffed out of the chimney.

Violet liked saunas, but not the excessive heat she knew others enjoyed. And since all the girls took a sauna together, she knew she had to endure the blistering heat, or just get in, wash quickly, and get out of the sauna as quick as she could.

Some called the sauna "Finnish bliss," others called it the "sanctuary of Finland." Whatever you called it, to Violet it was a means to an end—getting clean and visiting with Ann. However, others spent hours sitting on the benches discussing the affairs of the world.

Violet always had thought it was quite odd that people (sometimes they knew each other well, sometimes they didn't) actually enjoyed sitting on a skinny bench, in steaming heat, discussing matters near and dear, stark naked. It was just weird.

Yes, Violet liked the sauna, but she liked spending time with Ann even more. The girls ran giggling into the house, straight to the room Ann shared with her older sister Verna. Verna was rather bossy at times, but she was not in the room when the girls arrived, so the friends sat on the bed and started talking about important things.

"What did you do today?" tall, dark-haired Ann asked.

"Not much. Cleaned and did chores. How about you?" Violet asked in return.

"Same here," Ann shared. "But we have some new kittens in the shed! Want to see them?"

"Yes!" Violet answered as the girls bounced off the bed and ran back out the door and up the stairs to the shed.

One or two of the adults were saying something about running in the house, but the girls were long gone, the door banging shut behind them.

The kittens were so cute! Their soft fur and big eyes made them irresistible.

Later when the returned to the house, it was time for snacks. Ann's family provided homemade grape juice and mixed fruit. They also enjoyed the molasses cookies Lilith had made earlier in the day.

Ann's mom said it was time for the girls to go into the sauna, so they all tramped out the kitchen door and up to the sauna. Clothing was laid in careful piles as the girls undressed and banged into the bathing room. Soon the room filled with steam and giggling girls.

In Ann's sauna, the walls were made of sweet-smelling cedar. A stove glowed in the corner, upper and lower benches ran across the far wall. The girls took turns throwing water on the smooth rocks that surrounded the stove; they laughed as steam rolled to the ceiling and engulfed the room.

Snatching the dipper off the wall, Violet scooped some boiling water out of the hot water barrel and began filling her bucket for washing. She then turned on the faucet and added icy water to make it bearable. Suddenly, mischief danced in her eyes. She could not resist. Lilith and Verna were sitting on the top bench gossiping about boys— looking way too hot. Violet-the-Terrible smiled.

Swinging the hose, Violet looked at the older girls. "You girls look like you need some cooling down," she suggested to them sweetly.

Lilith glanced Violet's way. Understanding dawned. "Don't you dare!" she shrieked, her face contorting with disbelief and fury.

But Violet only laughed louder. She made a beautiful arc with the water coming out of the end of the hose and splattered the girls on the top bench. Their screams and horrible looking faces only egged Violet on. She and Ann laughed uncontrollable as the older girls cowered and tried to slide down off the benches, shrieking louder as their bare backsides scraped along the wooden seats.

As the older girls approached, Violet dropped the hose. Fast as cats, she and Ann ran out of the wet room and into the dry room of the sauna, dripping water everywhere.

They continued giggling as Verna, standing on the threshold, threatened them with a bucket of cold water. However, they knew she would not dare face the wrath of her father if she soaked the dressing room. Verna glared at them and slammed the door shut as she returned to her bathing.

Wrapping themselves in their towels, the younger girls subsided with giggles onto the benches.

"I guess we will just wait here until they're done," suggested Ann.

"Guess so," agreed Violet.

As they sat and waited and waited, suddenly their mischief almost didn't seem worth it.

"Yes, it was," shouted Violet, a little too loudly.

"What are you talking about?" queried Ann.

"Did you see their faces?" Violet began smiling again. "Yes, it was definitely worth it."

Ann agreed. The friends took turns mimicking the faces the older girls had made earlier as they were being drenched with the glacial water. Ann and Violet bent over sideways on the narrow benches as they rolled with laughter.

Best friends are the best, Violet decided.

Chapter Ten

Explosion!

Lilith came tearing into the barn yelling, "The tractor's on fire!"

"What! Where is it?" Adam shot as he quickly set down the bucket he was carrying and sprinted for the barn door, with Violet and Lilith right on his heels.

"The south field!" Lilith shouted back.

Adam hooked the fire extinguisher from the shop and charged past the house into the field behind, where the tractor sat smoking. Adam had a crooked gait, as one leg was shorter, due to his early illness. The girls galloped around him and beat him to the tractor. A small fire was burning in the engine. Adam rushed up to the tractor and quickly extinguished the flames.

He then whirled around to Lilith and demanded what had happened. She stammered out her story; Violet could see that she was shaking. Lilith explained that she was driving the tractor back to the shop, after feeding the hay to the cattle farther down in the field.

As she was driving, the tractor started spluttering and finally quit running. Lilith tried starting it a number of times to no avail. She then decided to see if it had run out of gas and took a match out of her pocket to check if the gas tank was empty. As she put the match flame close to the tank, it exploded and the fire ignited.

"Don't you know that gas will ignite when a flame is put to it?" Adam thundered.

Lilith replied sheepishly, backing away. "I guess I didn't think."

"You didn't think! You didn't think!" Adam echoed fiercely, face contorted with the effort. Violet wondered if a person could actually explode. "You could have been killed!" Adam stormed on. He turned and stomped away from the tractor, heading back to the barn.

When Adam had moved out of hearing, the girls looked at each other, eyes wide. "He's MAD!" Lilith observed through white lips.

"Mad as a hatter!" Violet agreed. "Mad, mad, mad. I thought he was going to burst!"

Some color returned to Lilith's lips and face. Her body relaxed.

Violet continued as the girls slowly made their way back to the barn, "Kind of like Rumpelstiltskin!" Then she danced around in a frenetic circle, flapping her arms, and making a wild face. Soon Lilith joined her. Twirling around, flailing their arms, the girls fell to the ground in a laughing heap.

"What's going on out there?" Adam boomed out the barn door, from across the yard.

Caught, the girls looked at each other, eyes wide.

"We tripped," Violet called to him, after a short pause.

"Hurry up Violet. We have calves to feed," Adam called loudly, turning to go back into the barn.

Lilith and Violet jumped up to do as he said. Violet glanced at Lilith as she helped her shut the gate. Lilith still looked a little scared. Chores done, Lilith hurried into the garage to get ready for school. Violet went up to the barn to help her dad finish feeding the calves, even though she really did not want to get anywhere near him.

Each morning, Adam brought two buckets of hot water up to the barn to mix with milk replacer powder to feed the calves. He had placed a four-foot long wooden block on the ground to set the buckets on for mixing. As Violet entered the barn, she saw Adam was filling the feeding pails with water and adding the powder. He turned slightly, seized the hand-made metal whisk off its nail on the wall, and began beating the mixture. Violet could tell he hadn't cooled down yet. Whisk, whisk, whisk! She wished it wasn't her turn in the barn this morning, but then quickly changed her mind. Better her than Lilith.

"She could have been killed," Adam repeated his earlier statement.

Violet only nodded, now feeling bad for both Lilith *and* Adam.

When Adam was done mixing, he took two pails and left one for Violet. Picking up the pail, she followed her dad down to the pen where the young calves were waiting for their breakfast. The young calves lived in stalls, chained to the wall. The chains were long enough so they could lie down comfortably and eat the hay that was left for them each morning and night. Their stalls had been scraped out earlier and new shavings had been put down for them to lie on during the day. They had been given some grain and hay in their little wooden boxes that were fastened to the front of each stall.

Violet drew in the crisp smell of the wood shavings that was used as clean bedding for the calves in the big old barn. When the shavings ran low, a big truck came and dropped off a fresh load from the mill.

Every morning and night Adam opened a little door, in each pen, to the outside of the barn and pitched out all of the fresh manure into piles. Periodically he would load the manure into the manure spreader and spread it over the fields for fertilizer. The pastures were always lush and green. After the manure was cleaned out of the pens, the kids would take a big round metal bin or two five-gallon buckets filled with the wood shavings to each pen and throw it around so the growing calves would have fresh places to lie.

As Violet waited for the calves to finish drinking the milk from the bucket, she thought about the sweet-smelling shavings, and remembered one of the few accidents that had happened on the farm. Just last year her oldest sister Sharon had gotten the first three fingers of her left hand cut off to the first knuckle as she was cleaning the shavings off the back of the truck. Scraping a few particles of shavings off the back of the truck, somehow her fingers were cut by a moving part. Violet curled her own fingers at the thought. She felt really bad for Sharon.

Everyone was so shaken up by this incident. Violet was not in the barn at the time, but she remembered Adam running into the house shouting, "Hannah, Hannah, we need to get

Sharon to the hospital, now! Her fingers have been cut!" They found the cut-off parts of her fingers that had fallen into the shavings, put them in a cup of water, and raced to the hospital. Lilith sat in the back with Sharon, holding her bandaged hand. Later, Sharon said her fingers didn't hurt; they just throbbed at this point—God's natural anesthesia at work. Later, Lilith said there was blood everywhere.

The hospital was a good hour away, but Adam got there in record time. Clomping down the hall in barn boots, he tried to get the help that Sharon needed. The hospital did not have the proper equipment or staff to help Sharon, so they loaded back into the vehicle, and headed to a bigger hospital in a larger city. Finally, they got to the right place, but the surgeon did not recommend trying to re-attach the fingers. Instead, he stretched Sharon's skin over the ends of her fingers and stitched them up as best he could. What an ordeal!

Sharon's fingers left Violet's mind as she looked around "5-pen" as they called this particular area where the youngest calves lived. Violet hooked the pail on the rack that was built to hold the buckets, but continued to hold onto the bucket as the calf hungrily worked the nipple on the pail to get the milk.

Becoming impatient, the calf bumped the pail with his head. Violet was glad she was holding the bucket; otherwise, milk would have spilled everywhere and she did not want to know what Adam would have said after what had already happened this morning.

Violet was also glad the first frost had come and all of the flies were gone. She glanced up and noticed the fly strips completely full of flies. She hated the flies that continually buzzed around the calves and crawled into their eyes and noses—laying their maggot-eggs. Disgusting! shivered Violet.

She looked over at the little calf in the next stall. He was so cute! Her dad said he thought it was a Charolais; a kind of calf they rarely got on the farm. He was Violet's. All hers. When he had come to the farm, Violet had asked her dad if she could have him. Adam said that would be okay, but to remember that he would be butchered when he got older. That seemed a long way off to Violet, so she didn't worry about it too much.

Each day she went to the barn, petted him, and brushed his soft fur. His coat was white with very light brown patches. Violet thought he was very special; she was working on an art project of her little calf. She had used stiff paper and had colored it just like her calf. Then she had cut Styrofoam cups down, painted them tan, and had used them for his hooves. The project was coming along nicely. Her little calf turned his head and looked at her with his beautiful brown eyes. Violet smiled back.

Adam and Violet finished feeding the rest of the calves and then Violet took the pails and whisk out of the barn to wash with Clorox and water. Adam insisted on everything being properly sterilized and put back in its rightful place.

As she finished up with the pails, she noticed quite a few kittens still licking milk out of the metal dish that was their feeding pan. Cats were everywhere! It was always a special adventure to try to find where the mama cats were keeping their babies. Since the kittens were born blind and pretty much hairless, they were kind of ugly at first. However, by the time they were toddling around in the barn, they were absolutely adorable as they stumbled and staggered about! Just teeny cute fur balls.

Violet stooped and picked up a little calico kitten that was rolling around with a piece of hay. Stroking the kitten's belly, she tried to tickle his chin. The wild kitten hissed and scratched Violet's hand. "Ouch!" She exclaimed, pulling her hand back. She accidently dropped the kitten, which quickly rolled over and ran away. So much for petting that cranky kitten, Violet grumbled as she licked her bleeding finger.

Sometimes the kittens got water and milk replacer to drink, other times they got milk straight from the cow. Twice a day their cow Ida was let into the barn to be milked. Clambering into the barn, she heaved herself up into the stall, poking her head into a stanchion where she ate hay while Adam milked her. Sometimes Ida seemed to purposely step on Adam's foot. He responded with a shout and a whack to her backside.

The kittens did not seem to mind the commotion; they just sat and waited patiently until Adam was done milking. He would then pour a little of the frothy milk into their pan before bringing the pail into the house to be strained and put into gallon jars. Sometimes the family used all of the milk, but at other times there was plenty left over to sell to the neighbors. One of the neighbors' jars always came back smelling suspicious to Hannah. She couldn't figure out why the jar smelled so funny.

Violet hurried out of the barn, latched the door, and walked over to rinse her boots in the rain bucket. She knew she needed to wash up and get ready for school quickly because the bus would be coming soon. Violet wondered what her dad was going to do about the charred tractor. To Violet, it actually did not look too bad. She hoped the whole thing would blow over quickly.

Yeah, the match thing was really dumb, but Violet too, was glad Lilith didn't get hurt.

Chapter Eleven

School, Butterflies, and Knobby Knees (aka – boys)

Violet quickly changed her clothes, washed up, and finished getting ready for school. Gulping oatmeal, brushing teeth, and getting dressed. She called good-bye to Hannah as she hurried to the door. Almost forgetting it, she turned back and grabbed her lunch sack, then sprinted out the door—the bus would be coming soon and Violet liked to be ready on time.

Sharon was notoriously late for the bus; it was embarrassing for Violet when the driver had to wait for Stately Sharon, who usually came stroooolling down the driveway like the queen of Sheba, while everyone waited for her. Good grief! With Sharon in high school and riding a different bus, waiting for her was over. Thank goodness!

Arriving at the bus stop at the end of the driveway, the farm children had a custom of calling out their positions for getting on the bus. To be last, was no one's intent! The first one down to the bus stop at the end of the driveway called "yksi" the Finnish number one, "kaksi" was two, "kolme" - three, "nelja"– four, "viisi" – five, "kuusi" – six, and "seitseman" – seven. This avoided any squabbles. Since Violet was now the oldest in the family going to the school in their rural town, she really didn't care if she was first or last getting on the bus. Almost all grown up, she didn't need to play children's games. Besides, the Finnish words rather irritated her anyway. Guttural and ugly, that's what she decided.

Waiting for the bus, Violet and the others were careful to stay back from the road to avoid being hit by any passing cars or trucks.

Today, they heard a big rig coming down the long hill. Soon, the log truck came storming into view, Jake brakes drumming, racks swaying around the curves. Then. . . whoosh, it flew by the waiting children. The wind from the large vehicle slammed against their bodies, pigtails flew back, and skirts became kites caught in the wind. How to get the drivers to blow their horns was a favorite game. Making pumping motions with their arms almost always worked and today was no exception. Broooonk! The horn blasted loud and long. Little kids jumped up and down in glee. Grinning, even Violet was pleased.

After the truck had passed, they children heard the bus coming; they lined up in readiness. Opening the door, the driver smiled a welcome. Not hesitating a bit, Eva charged up the stairs. The others followed and quickly found seats. Pew! Filling her nostrils, the smell of cigarette smoke disgusted Violet. It seemed their driver, Mrs. Ham, had enjoyed one last cigarette before the noisy kids filled her bus.

Where to find a seat was not a problem, as the farm kids were the first ones on the bus. Violet sat toward the back with the other big kids. Besides the cigarettes, Mrs. Ham was the coolest driver ever. Like this morning—she was driving without the interior lights on—the kids hummed with excitement.

Driving a little farther down the road to the turn-around, Mrs. Ham steered the bus in, bumping through ruts. To avoid being bounced out of her seat, Violet hung on to the bench in front of her. She was always afraid the driver might back up over the steep edge and the bus would go crashing down through the woods. Thank goodness, it never happened.

The bus started slowly back up the road to pick up the other kids. Soon, they stopped at the Hills'. Cam Hill was one grade younger than Violet and always sat right behind her on the bus. Every day. Violet knew he had a crush on her, but he rarely said a word to her, he just dropped a pack, or two, or three of gum into her seat. Every morning!

She had found out that his grandma worked at a store in California and sent the gum to Cam and his family, which he then shared with Violet. This morning, just like every morning, Violet said, "Thanks Cam" and that's as far as their romance (if you could even call it that, reflected Violet) ever went. However, the gum was good to chew and was a great bargaining tool with the younger children. Yup, Violet was definitely glad for Cam and the gum.

Continuing for another 45 minutes down narrow curvy roads, picking up other kids, the bus bounced its way to school. At times, when it rained really hard, the country roads would be covered with water. Whooosh! The large bus would slowly trundle through the sea created in lowlands. Sometimes Violet thought the bus might start floating and turn over in the deep water. To be trapped inside, unable to escape frightened her. However, that never happened either.

Nearing the school, the bus slowly climbed the last hill as the school buildings rose into view. Nestled in the fir trees, the school looked cozy and cheery. Butterflies always took wing in Violet's stomach as the bus lumbered into the schoolyard. Violet didn't know if she was excited or nervous, but it was probably a combination of both. The big bus swayed and groaned as it lurched into the parking lot. "Pshooo!" The bus stopped and the brake was set. Time to disembark.

The butterflies fought for flight. Grrr! Why does this always happen? Violet questioned.

Rubbing her tight belly, Violet prepared to streak out the door and fly up the pathway to the school building. Impatiently she waited her turn. She didn't know if it was the anticipation of a brand-new day, the opportunity to see friends, or just plain old jitters, but her churning stomach annoyed her. Not stopping to contemplate further, Violet bolted out the door and rushed to her classroom. She often wondered if she would throw up on the bus, but thank goodness, that never happened either!

As she settled into her seat and waited for the rest of the students to arrive, the butterflies subsided and Violet considered the day. School was fun for Violet. She loved the new classrooms with the sun streaming in the windows. She appreciated the big bulletin board that the teacher let her help decorate for the changing seasons. She prized the sink with the water that sprayed out like a fountain when she washed her hands. The smells of paper, pencils, and markers also enticed Violet's senses.

In addition, sometimes she even loved what she was learning! It was fun gaining knowledge of The English language and learning about its various parts. It was a challenge to dissect sentences and to see if she could get everything right.

Even mechanical drawing and math were fun. Art was usually enjoyable and PE was especially cool. Yup! Violet enjoyed almost everything about school. However, it really bothered her when some kids picked on others. Violet always tried to be nice to people and especially those who seemed to get pushed around. She hated it when some kids were so mean and other kids just seemed to take it. If it were up to her, she would make sure everyone was treated fairly and the meanies were punished! Bam! She would lock them all in a room together and let them pick on each other. That would serve them right!

Ringing, the bell signaled the start of the school day. The pupils who were still standing in the foyer ambled to their desks and Mrs. Jeffers took attendance and gathered the lunch tally. Pleased, Violet was asked to bring the papers to the main office. She put on her coat and ran outside with the envelope gripped in her hand.

As she headed down the paved path through the woods, the sun sparkled on the tall evergreen trees. Gorgeous! Noticing some icy patches, Violet slowed down and continued more carefully. Shivering in the cool morning air, Violet realized she should have grabbed her jacket. Reaching the bottom of the hill, she quickened her step; she did not want to miss much of the up-coming lesson.

She hurried past the playground, remembering how she used to love climbing on the monkey bars and riding the merry-go-round. Some of the kids would hook their legs through the bars on the merry-go-round and hang down and out as it went faster and faster. Violet couldn't do that since she always had to wear a dumb ol' skirt to school.

Walking the familiar path, Violet remembered when she was a couple years younger. She and her friend, Cindy, used to ever-so-casually stand by the path waiting for the big kids to walk past on their way to help in the kitchen. They waited for one boy in particular—Matt Roth.

Matt was tall, nice, and very good-looking. Both of the girls had a crush on him; however, Violet thought she had first dibs since he was a friend of her older brother and had actually been to her house. In fact, they had bred their pony with Matt's pony and then Crow Hopper, their black sassy baby was born. In Violet's mind, that sealed the deal for sure—she definitely held the right to crush on Matt!

Continuing on, Violet ran past the "big wall." Through the years, she had played hours of handball against the wall. When she was in the fifth and sixth grades, some of the teachers and all the kids used to play handball every recess. Huge, the wall was perfect. However, there was a challenge. The apron of concrete at the base of the wall followed the ground and dipped down, about 18 feet out, so whoever was on that side had better be a good strong player! The kids played in teams. Whoever was in the front of the line picked someone to be his or her partner. Being a tough player, Violet got picked a lot. The teachers also got picked for partners and so did Sam—he was really good.

Violet thought Sam was pretty much good at everything. In sixth grade, he helped her make a macramé plant hanger. It was their art assignment and Violet could not figure out how to properly braid it so that it twisted nicely, as it should. All she kept coming up with was a big clump of brown string that looked like a mop head. So, Sam helped her. How he could see out past his long eyelashes puzzled Violet. He also had gorgeous green eyes and the cutest smile. Sam was. . . . Well, never mind.

Coming back to the present, Violet clutched the papers and continued to the office. She entered the elementary building quietly and walked up the ramp to the office. "Blam!" Violet jumped as the old door shut heavily behind her.

Steadying herself, she continued to the office and gave her papers to the secretary Mrs. Barb. She had worked at the school forever. "Hello Violet, thanks for the records." Mrs. Barb smiled.

She's as old as the hills, but nice, noted Violet. "You're welcome," is what came out of her mouth as she turned and hurried back out the door. She tried not to look at the principal's office, or to think about what had happened to bring her there when she was in the third grade.

But, once she started thinking about it, the memory wouldn't stop coming. Violet hated it when that happened. It was like summer-warmed lubricant pooling out of her dad's grease gun. It just gushed out in a huge pile! The harder she tried not to think about something, the more she thought about it!

She ran hard across the playground as the memory chased her.

George West had really been a turd. She knew it was not Christian to dislike him so intensely, but she did. He thought he was the smartest and the best at everything. One day he was acting more awful than usual, so when Violet was standing in line after him to get a drink of water, she ever-so-gently tapped his head while he was bent over at the drinking fountain.

She only thought to get the water to squirt up his nose, but the baby went and bumped his head on the fountain and got a bloody nose! Of course, he went whining to their teacher, Mrs. Gray who put on her spectacles and peered at Violet in surprise. Violet rarely got in trouble, but this time she was sent to the principal's office! Violet had never been sent to the principal's office—it was terrifying. She could hardly believe this was happening to her!

The awful memory continued. It was the end of the day, so Mrs. Gray told Violet to take her things with her. Gathering her lunch sack, papers, and books, and trying hard not to let the threatening tears seep out of her eyes, Violet slowly trudged to the office. She blinked and thought angry thoughts about George. What a big baby! She would not cry like that turd! The door banged shut behind her as she trudged up the hall, wondering what was going to happen.

Too soon, she reached the office, slowly opened the door, and shuffled in. The unique smell of the office greeted her—papers, mold, and antiseptic from the first aid supplies. Mrs. Barb looked at her; if Violet had been herself, she would have noticed a sympathetic look. But, Violet was not herself; she was bristling with injustice.

Banging down into a seat in the office, she jostled her books, peechee, and her leftover lunch on her lap. She clutched an orange in her fist; she was planning to eat it on the bus on the way home. Fidgeting, she waited impatiently for the principal to come and talk to her. Oh no! The buses were lining up in front of the school. Would she miss her ride home? And then what? Violet did not even want to think about it!

Finally arriving, the stern-looking principal seated himself across the desk from Violet. His shirt was crisp and white, even though it was the end of the day. He looked disapprovingly through his round spectacles at Violet. She tried to look sorry, but she wasn't!

The principal droned on and on, preaching to Violet about what an awful disrespectful thing she had done, wondering how such a nice girl could be so naughty. Violet did not know what came over her, but as the principal continued in his nasal offensive tone, she got madder and madder. Her grip on the orange tightened, she felt the juice begin to dribble on her skirt.

The temptation was too great, her feelings overwhelmed her, and before she could stop herself, Violet threw her orange right at the principal's white clean shirt! The fruit splattered and rolled onto his desk. He sat there stunned for a while (and so did Violet!). Crimson fury soon engulfed his face. His eyes bulged behind the round lenses. "You've gone too far!" he barked at Violet. "I'm calling your mother."

Violet knew this was all an awful mistake. How did it get to this point she wondered. Why did that dumb George have to be in front of me in line anyway? I hate him, she thought with feral vengeance. This is all his fault!

In the back of her mind, she knew it was no one's fault but her own, but she was not ready to admit that yet. Agony filled her chest and rose into her throat. How would she ever endure this torture?

When her mother arrived at the school and got her from the office, Violet silently slid into the long blue station wagon (their vehicle at the time). Hannah talked to Violet all the way home, finishing with, "What do you think your father is going to say?"

Violet clenched her fist in her skirt, feeling the sticky orange juice; she thought she was going to throw up. What *would* Adam say? Her mother was one thing, but her father was something else.

Arriving home, she was sent upstairs to wait until her dad got home from work. That was the worst! Violet refused to think about the humiliation that she had gone through, listening to people lecture her for something that was not entirely her fault! It was awful! No, it was more than awful.

When Adam got home and heard the story, he really didn't hit the roof, but instead, he was very calm. Violet waited for the verdict.

She was told to go and "ask for forgiveness" from her teacher! What?! Violet knew the way her church "asked for forgiveness" was different from how other people did things. How would old Mrs. Gray know how to respond? How would Violet bear this humiliation? What was she going to do? Maybe the world would end in the night and all of this would go away.

She thought about it for the rest of the evening, waking at night thinking about it, and all the next day at school it wouldn't leave her mind. Torment was her ever-present companion.

Through the day, she tried and failed to get up courage. Finally, it was her last chance. Violet's classmates were doing their final lesson. She finished early and slowly approached Mrs. Gray's desk, heart pounding, hands damp with worry. "I'm sorry for what I did yesterday!" Violet blurted out.

Mrs. Gray smiled and graciously replied, "It's ok; I like it when little girls are sweet." Embarrassed, but vindicated for the moment, Violet wheeled and returned to her seat, gathering her belongings in preparation to go home.

But now, how was she going to tell Adam about it? Because Violet knew he would ask.

She thought of all the ways she could get around the fact that she did not actually "ask for forgiveness." Nor had Mrs. Gray said the special "forgiveness" phrase that Violet's church used. She knew she was going to lie to her dad if necessary. She also knew it was a sin, but at this point, she told herself, she really did not care.

Sure enough, during barn chores that evening, Adam was mixing the water and milk replacer for the calves. Violet was standing nearby waiting. Calves bawled for their supper and the kittens were finishing licking the milk out of their dish. Not missing a beat in his mixing, still bent over, Adam said, "So, did you ask for forgiveness from Mrs. Gray?"

Violet felt a little uneasy, she slid her boot across the mixture of shavings and hay in front of her and replied, "Yes."

"And what did she say?" returned Adam.

"She said 'I like it when little girls are sweet,'" mumbled Violet.

Adam nodded and continued stirring the contents of the bucket. And that was the end of it. Except for Violet knew she did not do exactly what Adam had told her to do and she had lied about it. Another sin to add to her list.

"Yuck" Violet muttered aloud, when the memory finally subsided.

These thoughts had taken her all the way to the base of the hill winding up to the seventh and eighth grade building. Violet, skirt twisting in her legs, ran all the way up the hill, thankful she didn't slip on the ice, but glad to be escaping the shame of her experience of years ago. She was glad she was all grown up now and never was sent to the principal's office again!

With relief, she arrived back at her classroom and slid into her seat.

Today was Wednesday. Violet loved Wednesdays! They had Physical Education on Mondays, Wednesdays, and Fridays. And Violet liked PE! She was good at PE. She was especially happy they got to change into shorts for PE. It was a welcome escape from the dumb dresses she had to wear to school every single blasted day—Adam's orders. When I grow up, I'm never wearing a dress again, Violet fervently vowed.

Once the students had changed into their PE attire, they gathered in the big gym. Oh yeah! Today's going to be great! Violet reflected. They were in the middle of a badminton challenge; Sam and she were partners. Winning partners, she gloated in her mind.

Anxiously, she waited for the boys to come out of their locker room. The butterflies were in her stomach again. Sam and Stewart were walking together. She tried not to act as if she was looking, but couldn't help herself. Sam was so cute! Well, Stewart was cute too, but Sam was nicer. Violet also tried not to look at the boys' legs. They really look like chicken legs, she thought. All skinny and knobby and white. Ewww. Why did boys have such hideous legs?

Soon Mr. Kay came out of the locker room. He was always smiling and chatting. Violet liked him a lot. "Hey Vibes!" Mr. Kay called out when he saw Violet.

She smiled and waved, hoping she wasn't turning eight shades of red. Urggh! Why does that have to happen? she moaned silently. Nice teachers who embarrassed her and cute boys with knobby knees who confused her. Life was perplexing!

Violet trudged outside, following the rest of the kids who were gathering on the curb around Mr. Kay. Brightly, the sun shone from the radiant blue sky. Violet felt happier in the warm sunshine; she hated the gray skies and rain. Mr. Kay was talking, explaining what they were going to do in PE class today. The birds circling in the tall evergreen trees distracted Violet. She loved watching the birds flit from one branch to another, chasing each other as they played.

Violet was crouched on the curb next to Mr. Kay as he talked. His strong bare legs were directly in front of her. The birds lost their draw as Violet noticed the sun glistening on the curly hair growing profusely on those legs. The hair both drew her and disgusted her. Her hand, seemingly on its own volition, reached out and pulled one of the hairs on his leg! It was soft, yet wiry. Gross! Her hand fell back to her lap, as if scorched.

Violet was almost as surprised as Mr. Kay! He jumped a little and then smiled at her. He liked Violet and was used to young teenagers and their strange behavior. Violet's friend Dee was sitting next to her. She laughed as Violet's cheeks turned scarlet. Why, oh why, do I always do such stupid things?! Violet groaned to herself. She wished she could crumble into the curb.

PE class continued and after awhile Violet didn't think of the hair incident again. Not until they were riding the bus home. Then Dee started telling a bunch of people about what happened. Violet was shocked. "It was no big deal!" she exclaimed. "Even Mr. Kay didn't think it was a big deal."

"Ha! Wait til mom finds out about this!" Sharon teased. Even though Sharon went to another school, the older kids rode a bus from the high school and were joined by the elementary kids at the end of the day. Would she ever be truly rid of Sharon-the-Terrible? Violet fumed.

"You wouldn't!" Violet shouted over the hubbub on the bus.

"Just watch me!" yelled the grinning Sharon.

Violet wanted to scream! She also wanted to slug Sharon right in the gut.

She's so mean, stormed Violet to herself. I hate her!

The big bus rumbled on, unperturbed by Violet's raging emotions. The bus swung around the corners, and groaned down the hills. Too soon, they arrived home.

To Violet, it seemed as if Sharon practically *ran* up the driveway, intent on her evil deed. She couldn't wait to get Violet in trouble. Well, it really wasn't that she was mean. She just liked to watch Violet squirm; she thought it was funny.

Violet did not want to face her mother and the coming lecture so she snuck into the house after all the others had gone in. Quickly, she ran upstairs, changed, and dashed back out before Hannah could get ahold of her. She took her sweet time doing her chores; tonight she seemed to find all kinds of things that needed extra attention. So, it wasn't until Adam got home that Violet finally went back into the house.

They usually ate promptly once Adam arrived home, so Violet washed up and headed down the hall to find everyone already at the table.

She slid into her spot.

"How was your day, Violet?" her dad asked from his place immediately to her right.

Suspecting added meaning, Violet was a little short and cocky. "Just fine," she said. "Just *absolutely* fine!"

Now why did I have to say that? She questioned herself. Now he will think something's up for sure.

And that's exactly what happened.

"What's going on here?" Adam asked, looking around the table.

Silence and shrugs answered him.

And then three-year-old Gloria spoke into the silence. "Violet pulled the teacher's hair."

"What?! You pulled the teacher's hair?" Adam and Hannah chorused, turning incredulous gazes to Violet, who did not seem to hear them.

"You big stinking pig!" Violet was hollering at Sharon.

"I didn't say anything!" Sharon hollered back.

"Girls!" Hannah admonished.

Adam now turned to Gloria. "What are you talking about Gloria?" he questioned her.

With all the yelling and commotion, Gloria started crying and blubbered, "I heard Sharon and Lilith talking in the bedroom." She wiped snot on her sleeve and continued to snuffle.

Adam now turned to Violet. "Is it true?" he questioned again. "*What* did you do?"

Violet-the-Anguished refused to let the threatening tears fall. She quickly explained, realizing it all sounded so much worse than it really was.

When she was done with the telling, both Adam and Hannah sat in stunned silence.

Adam shook his head. "Let's say the prayer," he sighed. "Violet it's your turn."

"God is great, God is good, and we thank him for our food. By his hand we must be fed, give us Lord our daily bread. In Jesus' name, Amen." Violet mumbled.

The family began passing the dishes and filling their plates. Hannah opened her mouth to say something to Violet. Adam looked at Violet, then at Hannah, and shook his head slightly. Hannah stopped talking and passed the potatoes.

Violet wished she was sitting at the North Pole instead of right next to Adam. She waited for the boom to fall on her. Instead, something strange started happening. Violet glanced at her dad. He was shaking. She blinked and looked again. He was shaking because he was trying not to laugh! What in the world?!

Now Hannah started to smile and soon most of the children joined in, relieved. And then, they didn't even try to hold back; everyone was laughing until tears came. Violet sat in humiliated silence as long as she could, then she jumped up, and fled to her room.

Throwing herself onto her squeaky bed, she kicked some clothes off her bed with a vengeance. Violet groaned. Life seemed so difficult; so awkward! She pounded the bed. She groaned again and rubbed her eyes. It's not fair, she told herself. It's just not fair! One dumb little thing and the whole world has to know about it. And laugh at me! It's not fair at all.

After some time, she rolled over onto her belly and looked out the window. The leaves on the trees waved in the wind, calming her raging spirit. She tucked her hands under her chin. Sometimes life was truly awful. Horrible! Why did she do such stupid things? Why did her family have to be so mean?

Sighing, she found her pillow, squished it under her chest, and settled in for a reverie with the dancing leaves outside her window. The curtains fluttered in the breeze, responding to the wind blowing through the open window. Sometimes life was truly awful, she reckoned. But, she knew there were other times when it . . . wasn't. She sighed again.

There were times when the words from the stories she read played like soft waterfalls in her mind. When the characters came to life and teased her with grand ideas. Times when she felt she could step into another world. Times when the branches of the trees and the pattern of the good things lulled her. Soothed her.

She rolled onto her side and hugged her second pillow to her. Her eyes closed. There were times when learning at school was actually fun. And there were times when Sam and she played badminton. Times when Sam looked at her . . . smiled with his knowing eyes, and . . .

Never mind. Sam was one secret she was definitely keeping to herself.

Chapter Twelve

Traveling Salesgirls

Tired and hungry, Lilith and Violet trudged on.
Selling Christmas cards from a flyer they got
through the school was hard work. Neighbor
after neighbor said they already had cards.
Tight wads! Violet thought. As if they couldn't
use a few more cards! Card sales were not
going so well.

For many days now, starting a few weeks
before Thanksgiving, they had walked miles
up the road, going from house to house.
Smiling as nicely as they could, trying to make

some money to get the exciting gifts that were offered in the brochure. Violet couldn't decide between a Kodak camera or a set of pens and markers. She would have to decide soon.

Today was the last day they could sell cards in order to get everything turned in on time. The wind blew cold through their jackets. On they walked, buttoning their coats against the chilly breeze.

Just one mile from home, they stopped at a favorite neighbor's house. Many of the kids in the family had worked for her over the years. Yard work, house cleaning, and house sitting. The kids all liked her. Margaret's standards were high, but the rewards were great.

In fact, before the school year had started, Margaret had taken Violet shopping for brand new school clothes! They had even gone out to lunch. Arriving to pick up Violet from the farm in her long black luxury car, Margaret seemed like royalty visiting the local sharecroppers. To Violet, the whole day had seemed like a dream. Something make-believe. Yup, that was a special day.

However, (and she never told kind, but stately Margaret) somehow the cashmere sweater she had so generously bought for Violet shrunk in the wash. It now fit Violet's three-year-old sister! So soft and pretty, now worn by a child. Violet missed her treasured sweater. Well, how was she supposed to know how to take care of *cashmere,* for Pete's sake? . . . I guess I could have read the label, she considered with a frown. She pushed the memory back.

As Lilith and Violet descended the sharp driveway leading to the house, Violet glanced over at the trailer house on the edge of the property. Last year, she had stayed nights with the old grandma who lived there, before she passed. That was kind of fun, but the experience definitely let Violet know she would not be taking care of old people when she grew up. No ma'am. The things Violet had to do were sometimes too much to even think about. Well, anyway, the grandma had been kind. Caring for the old lady was difficult, but Violet *did* like to watch the forbidden TV shows with her. Lawrence Welk and his bands were amazing. The singing and dancing opened up a completely undiscovered world to Violet. Pretty dresses, dance steps, and music. Mmm. But now, Lawrence Welk and the dancing women faded away.

Continuing down the drive, Violet glanced out across the enormous green pasture. Tucked up next to a great tree-covered ridge, the field looked magnificent. Even a small stream flowed through the property. Adam's cattle grazed contentedly. A few looked up as the girls approached and then went back to ripping out the grass with their big teeth. Soon Adam and the kids would come to get the cattle and take them home for the winter. Rounding up the summer-wild cattle was always a rodeo.

Lilith probably would stay home from the round-up. She really wasn't a farmer at all, Violet surmised. Especially when it came to rounding up cattle. One time at home in the barnyard, when she was supposed to be guarding an opening, she got scared and scrambled up the chicken house steps when the cattle charged her way. What the rip! That's why you made noise and swung around big sticks. So now, Lilith stayed in the house during cattle round-ups. There was no use having her around if she was just going to run away!

Violet also remembered a snowy night just last year when she and her older sisters had spent a few magical hours zooming over the snow in that same field. Margaret and her husband, Sparks had a couple of snowmobiles that they said the kids could use after one of their rare snowstorms. Violet had never ridden a snowmobile before. What an experience! Clear and brilliant, the night sparkled in the moonshine. Flying over the pasture, snow swirling in their wake—it all felt so incredibly free and wild. Violet hoped it snowed again this year.

Arriving at Margaret's door, the girls rang the bell. Pulling aside the curtain and peering through the window at them, recognition dawned on Margaret's face and she smiled. "Hello girls, what are you up to?" she inquired kindly as she swung open the door.

"We're selling Christmas cards," Violet explained.

"Would you like to look at our catalog?" Lilith chimed in.

"Well, sure," Margaret replied. "But only if they get here in time for me to send them out for Christmas," she continued, speaking through red lipstick.

"Oh absolutely!" Violet, salesgirl extraordinaire, assured her. "Yes, we will send the order in tomorrow."

Waving them in, Margaret offered a Coke. The girls smiled and nodded their heads. Coke in individual cans was a treat the girls only got at Margaret's house. They all settled around the kitchen table.

She sure is taking her time, Violet thought to herself as Margaret pored over the catalog. Finally, she made her selection. Carefully, Lilith wrote down the order. It was the most expensive order the girls had made! Dollar signs flashed in Violet's mind. Well, more like the points that were attached to the dollar amounts. Margaret had chosen shiny red cards, complete with their name embossed on the front. The cards would be stunning.

"Bring them over as soon as they come!" Margaret admonished the girls as they made their way down the concrete steps. "I will be waiting!"

"Oh, we will, we will!" the girls chorused, running up the driveway. Coats and skirts flapped in the breeze.

Out of sight of Margaret, they grinned at each other. "Oh! Now I can get that camera I wanted!" crowed Violet.

"And I can get that desk organizer," smiled Lilith, ever the organized lady.

The girls ran all the way home. They sat right down at the dining room table, calculated their earnings, and finished the order form. Putting everything in a large envelope, the girls felt excited about receiving the items they had earned.

Two weeks passed. Every day they diligently checked the mail. No cards. Day after day, they came home from school and pulled open the mailbox at the end of the driveway. Still no cards. It was now only two weeks until Christmas. The girls were starting to get nervous.

Margaret called asking, where were her cards? The girls told her they would call the company. Hannah made the call for them. They were assured the cards were in the mail. Finally, nine days before Christmas the errant cards arrived. Hannah drove the girls around, delivering the cards to the angry neighbors.

Boy, this didn't turn out so well, Violet mused as yet another unhappy customer frowned at them.

Dejected, the girls finished their deliveries; they rode home in gloom. Rain slapped at the windshield.

Arriving home, Violet unpacked her camera. Well, it's not my fault those dumb cards came late, she huffed to herself. She loaded the film into her Kodak 110 camera and put the square flash bulb into the proper slot. She had never had a camera before and she felt pretty darn cool. She positioned her favorite things on a chair in her room and took a picture. Running down the stairs and out the door, Violet considered what to photograph.

Miraculously, the rain had stopped. She took some more pictures outside—cats, Frisky, the barnyard. This is fun! Violet thought. She felt almost all grown up. It wasn't every 13-year-old who had a job and earned a camera. And, she was determined to enjoy it.

Unhappy customers or not, *she* had done her job and had a right to enjoy her reward.

Chapter Thirteen

Christmas

Christmas in the big white farmhouse just past milepost 27 was an exciting time of year.

After Thanksgiving, each family member's name was carefully written on a piece of paper and put in a hat. With much anticipation, everyone took turns drawing out a name, checking to be sure they had not drawn their own name. Papers were tucked into special places, not to be discovered, and the sneaking around began. Wish lists were made and taped up on a row of cupboards in the kitchen. Ever so casually, the wish lists were studied by others and items copied down.

Adam usually gave all the children some shopping money, and this year was no different. It kind of surprised Violet that during the year money was always scarce, but at Christmas, there seemed to be some extra. Maybe Adam had a special fund just for Christmas, she contemplated. Whatever the case, Violet was pleased. Because, gone was the money she had made from berry picking, and her meager weekly allowance barely covered her candy and art supplies.

All family members were busy with preparing presents. Hannah was extra busy, sewing clothes for the children—measuring, fitting, and stitching. The sewing machine clacked on, sometimes long into the night. Pieces of fabric and thread littered the floor. It was amazing what Hannah could do with a section of fabric and the old sewing machine.

Plans were made for a special time of opening gifts. This year Christmas Eve was chosen. The family always spent Christmas day at church. They ate their meals there and everything. In fact, Violet was usually tired of going to the services that lasted through New Year's Day. However, it was the custom of the church at the time and that is what they always did.

The little girls made red, green, and white paper chains, draping them from the high casings around door structures. Green boughs found their way indoors; Lilith tied them with red ribbons and placed them on the tables. Shiny blue, silver, red, and green paper was begged for at school; Violet triumphantly brought the paper home to cut out bells and other beautiful symbols of Christmas. Sharon hung Adam's old gray woolen socks along the large casing between the living and dining rooms.

The woodstove in the corner of dining room burned day and night. The wood box in the back porch was filled and emptied daily as the stove worked to keep the family warm.

Especially after working outside, the kids warmed their backsides along the edge of the stove. Hats, gloves, and jackets hung drying along the bricks that rose halfway up the wall around the back of the stove. The steamy moisture they exuded was a unique smell—barnyard aromas of hay and other things.

During Christmas preparations, barn smells mixed with the smell of baking bread, bubbling fudge, and prune tarts—all family favorites. Hannah made wonderful nisu—Finnish sweet bread laced with cardamom, especially good when warm and frosted.

Tonight Adam was making fudge after the barn chores were done. He was stirring and stirring and stirring the pot for a long time. Finally, it was finished, poured into a pan, and left to cool.

Adam called the children together and told them they were going to read in the living room. Violet received the news with mixed feelings. She liked listening to her dad read, but it took away from her own reading time and working on her art projects. However, he was getting close to finishing "The Dog of Flanders." So far, it had been good. Sad, but good. Violet did not like to cry in front of the others; she could usually hold her tears until she got to the safety of her comfortable squeaky bed.

Adam usually read the Bible or other Christian writings aloud. But sometimes, he read altogether different stories. Violet remembered "Heidi" and "Pilgrim's Progress." They had been sad too, in parts. After one night of reading, Violet and Lilith had accidently found each other crying in the dark back hallway. Violet loved that about the old farmhouse. Not the crying, but the hiding places, such as the back hallway. There were lots of interesting nooks and crannies in the old house. Like the closet in the back hallway. You could hide in there, under the old clothes, for a long time and no one would ever find you.

The upstairs closets were another matter. Early on, the kids were convinced real bears lived under the eaves in the long dark spaces. How the bears got in there, never occurred to the children when they were little. At the time, it was easy to believe the animals lived there, especially when bats sometimes came creeping in and flying around inside the house. If bats could get in, why couldn't bears? Violet now realized the error in her early thinking. But as a child, she had been terrified that the bears would come growling out at night.

Violet left the bats and bears, to gather in the living room with the rest of her family. She was tired. She leaned into the green and gold scratchy couch and closed her eyes. "The Dog of Flanders" ended—a sad tale of a strong bond between a boy and his dog. Love, that's what it was.

Done reading, Adam agreed to share the fudge. Licking the sweet confection off her spoon, Violet again contemplated the coming Christmas celebrations and then got ready for bed.

After school the next day, Sharon was making prune tarts, assisted by Hannah. She was going to bring them to her Home Economics class to share. The prunes were left to simmer on low until they were soft and sweet, sugar was added and dough was rolled. The intricate shapes of the prune tarts were cut by a kitchen gadget, a blob of prunes was dropped in the middle and every other point of the cut-out was tucked up to make a pretty star shape. Sugar was sprinkled on; then the tarts were baked, cooled, and eaten. The soft dough melted in the mouth and the prune filling was divine sweetness.

During the day, Hannah had made pies, bread, and casseroles to be brought to the church for the special Christmas services. They enjoyed some of these treats after school and at supper time.

Piling up, presents overflowed from behind the long couch that sat under the South-facing window. Violet thought it was somewhat strange to put all the presents behind the couch, but with the babies digging into things, it was necessary. The couch needed to be scooted farther out from the wall as more and more presents were added. Nametags were searched for clues, but no one wrote whom the gifts were from. People darted around, closing doors, and feverishly wrapping before peering eyes could see the purchased treasures.

Christmas Eve finally arrived. It was time to open the gifts! Finishing chores early, the family began gathering in the living room. Excitement snapped in the air. Sniffing the smell of hot cocoa, Violet hurried downstairs. The little kids buzzed around like bees.

Anticipation glowed from smiling faces.

"Where's Sharon?" Lilith wondered.

Eva ran to find her. "She's wrapping her presents," Eva soon reported back to the waiting family.

It figures, Violet grumped to herself. Last-Minute-Nelly-Pants-Sharon! She's slow as molasses in January.

The younger children hurried upstairs to carry Sharon's packages down for her. There were tons of them! The newspaper-wrapped gifts were added to the other gaily-wrapped packages. Finally, Sharon appeared; it was time. "Sorry I'm late," Sharon announced. "I got something for everyone."

Will miracles never cease? Violet marveled, rather unkindly. That was really nice of her. Humph.

All of the gifts were handed out; each person had a pile in front of them ready to be opened. Adam wanted the gifts opened one at a time— to be enjoyed, and the giver properly thanked. In addition, everyone could see what the others got. Youngest to oldest, the opening began.

Dolls, trucks, shoes, games, sweaters, books, hats, and nuts all found their way out of green and red paper. Squeals of delight and glad smiles sat in a circle around the braided living room rug. Piles of paper, ready for the hungry woodstove was stuffed in the corners. Adam put his new orange hunting cap right on his head. His cans of cashews lined the floor around his leg-less chair, (everyone knew Adam loved his midnight snack of cashews and peanut butter crackers).

Grandpa and Grandma had sent fudge, hats, and mittens for all the kids. Thank you notes would soon be in the mail to them.

After some time, the gift opening was over and the paper was piled in a box for burning. The children gathered their heaps of treasures and ran to their rooms to try on their special clothing.

Lilith had given Violet some very high-heeled sandals that looked fantastic with her gunny-sac look-alike dress she also received. She loved the long cable-knit cream-colored sweater—a gift from her mom. Altogether, her outfit looked marvelous, Violet decided as she twirled in front of her mirror. Never mind it was the middle of winter and the sandals should wait until summer, Violet was going to wear them to church on Christmas day, come snow, sleet, or most likely—rain!

Soon the family returned to the dining room for Christmas snacks and singing of some favorite Christmas songs. Happiness and thoughts of a Savior were in the hearts of all those who lived in the big white farmhouse.

After some time, the din died down as eyelids began to droop. Softly, the embers sparkled and burned in the woodstove. Dishes were piled in the sink, and "goodnights" were said.

The stockings still hung above the casement, filled with oranges and shelled peanuts and candy canes. Violet smiled. Some traditions are very good, she thought. The patterns of life, and love.

Slowly the room emptied, lights snapped off . . . and only the shadows remained.

Violet sleepily climbed the stairs and plopped down on her bed. The springs squeaked, welcoming her. Slowly undressing, she thought back over the day. Then she snuggled under her covers, wriggling into a comfortable position.

Christmastime, oh Christmastime, pattern of life indelible, Violet mused, changing the line from E.B. White's lake story. It seemed that no matter the little changes from year to year, the Christmas celebration was still the same overall. A sweet pattern of life. Closing her eyes to these intriguing thoughts, Violet slept.

And so, another year passed for the family living in the sprawling farmhouse, surrounded by trees and animals. Just around the corner waited the New Year and all the changes it was sure to bring to Violet and those she loved best.

The End